The Secret Diary of an Intimate Waxer

Mona Pearson

Editor: Anne Hamilton www.writerightediting.co.uk

Illustration and cover design: Arjan van Woensel

1st edition 2024

ISBN 978-1-0685946-1-8

Contents

CHAPTER ONE

Introduction

If you have ever had an intimate wax, you will know just what a terrifying prospect it is. Particularly the first time; you will rarely find yourself in quite such a vulnerable position. Meeting someone new is difficult enough without having to take your underwear off – especially if they are keeping theirs on.

There is no elegant way to climb on to a treatment bed when you are naked from the waist down: the strange sensation of the air on your nether regions, whilst your top half is fully clothed; lying with a towel draped over you, soon to be removed, revealing your bits in a surreal game of peek-a-boo. And as if the stress caused by partial nudity isn't enough, you also need to worry about hair being ripped from the most sensitive of areas. Even more insufferable you are obviously not looking too sharp down below, otherwise, why would you be getting waxed? You wouldn't cut the grass before you got the gardener in.

I am a waxer. Waxing is the only treatment I do, a job I came to by chance, but completely fell in love with. Six days a week I wage a war against body hair. I take it very seriously, but even after all these years it still makes me chuckle that I pay my bills and take my kids on holiday by ripping peoples' pubes out with hot wax. People come to me looking like 70's porn stars and leave looking like Hollywood starlets – between their legs, at least.

Without trying to sound big headed, I am very good at what I do. This is in large part down to technique, which I have practised and perfected over many years. Having waxed as many vaginas as Bernard Matthews has plucked turkeys, I pride myself on providing the best wax possible, in the quickest time possible.

Although a perfectly executed wax is a very important element of the treatment, it means nothing if the client is uncomfortable. This is where my special talent comes in handy: I have a natural ability to put people at ease; it's not something I learned and it's not forced. I like people and I find it easy to get along with just about everyone. I am also unashamedly open about everything, often to the embarrassment of my husband, who has, with surprising frequency, had to remind me that the waiter doesn't need our life-story when we are ordering our lunch. The most memorable occasion was whilst ordering monkfish tail, and me speculating as to how often my in-laws have sex – if at all?

I barely registered the waiter's look of horror as he looked to my husband to see his reaction. I was already laughing hysterically at how funny I was. I soon realised that nobody else found this amusing, which I took to mean they didn't understand the joke. I gladly explained that my mind had wandered to my mother-in-law's vagina, which I imagined looked like a monkfish – all rubbery with lots of teeth.

I assured my husband that I had seen enough vaginas to be able to speculate as to what his mother's might look like, and it would certainly explain the constant pained look on his father's face.

I often wonder if I have Tourette's, as I always seem to be saying inappropriate things out loud; the kind of things that most people wouldn't even think.

This has proved invaluable during my work, though, because saying the most bizarre things out loud disarms people. Each new client who lies on my bed, quickly forgets the awkwardness of the situation, as I happily tell them about comparing my mother-in-law's fanny to a deep-sea predator – or whatever else pops into my head.

You see, in a tense situation like an intimate wax, openness becomes contagious and is a wonderful thing. It's hard to tell exactly why people are so candid with me: the nature of the treatment? The client exposing their most private parts to me (literally)? My ability to put people at ease? Perhaps it's a combination of all three.

I think it also helps that I am not based in a high-street salon and all the footfall that goes with it. No, I work from an outbuilding in my back garden in the middle of suburbia. I have one treatment room, a small waiting area and a tiny bathroom. People come to my home, they walk past my kids playing in the garden and occasionally bump into my hubby, who has an office adjacent to my workroom. This helps them to relax and feel like part of the family.

It is all a perfect storm that leads to people regaling me with the most fantastical stories from their lives; stories they wouldn't dare tell anyone else – not their friends, their colleagues, or even their families. I often feel like a priest, my treatment room a confessional box, only there is no judgement and certainly no penance. I become more than a waxer; I am an ear to bend, a shoulder to cry on, a sounding board, a counsellor, an advisor, a friend – all rolled into one lean, mean, waxing machine.

As you can imagine, I have amassed a catalogue of stories over the years, some funny, some unbelievable, some weird, some inspiring, and some downright disgusting.

One of my clients, now a firm family friend, has told me for years that I should write a book – a diary, of sorts – of these stories. This is that book. A collection of individual stories and memories that make me laugh. There is no lesson to be learned, or moral to be taken from my diary. And in the interest of fairness, I have thrown in a large dollop of embarrassing tales from my own life; digressions of a waxer, if you like.

That said, discretion is a huge part of my business and I take it very seriously. Everything I am going to tell you has truly happened – sadly I don't have a vivid enough imagination to make even half of this stuff up. All names have been changed, and only secrets and lies already exposed have made it to the final cut, unless the client is dead or in prison.

This book might not be for you if you are easily offended, or of a weak disposition. And, as almost all the content consists of things that make me laugh, it is largely an immature affair. There is bad language, perverted pensioners, descriptive bodily functions – voluntarily and involuntarily – and even a dead body being massaged.

I always try to find the funny in any situation, as nothing quite soothes the soul as much as a good, long belly laugh. So, if you need a chuckle and have a strong stomach, then read on.

CHAPTER TWO

Edna and Bob

LOVE'S OLD DREAM...

When I was first starting out, having completed my training, but still earning my stripes, I worked mobile. It was a tedious affair, having to drag all my kit around house to house – folding treatment bed, wax pots, wax strips, cleanser, etc. I never refused a job, no matter how bad my back got lugging about the bulky bed, or how grimy the client's house looked from the outside. It was during these early days, I realised just how bizarre my new career was going to be.

One of my first regular clients was a lady called Edna, who was in her late seventies. Edna's husband, Bob, phoned to book her initial appointment. This immediately struck me as odd; I wondered what kind of man arranges his wife's waxing appointment. I didn't have to wonder for long, as Bob was more than happy to tell me how Edna's hair was causing his penis discomfort during their energetic lovemaking. I was impressed and surprised in equal measures at the thought of two septuagenarians having the energy and inclination to be having sex, let alone so frenetically as to cause friction burns. I wondered if some lube would be more useful than a wax – I made a mental note to check with my mother-in-law what she used, then thought better of it. Despite my concerns I arranged an appointment for Edna.

When I arrived at their house, it was an ex-local authority property that had been badly maintained. Overgrown, leaking gutters, rotten windowsills, and flaking paint on the front door. A sign of what was to come, I feared. Bob opened the door and on first appearance I found it hard to believe he could even find his penis under his massive belly, let alone use it to good enough effect to cause any sort of friction.

The inside of the house was as I expected: brown shag pile carpets, the vile colour masking God only knows what kind of horrors; nicotine stained walls; dust-covered ornaments; a forty-year-old Paisley patterned couch. The smell was indescribable, but I'm sure you can imagine. I pressed on, and set up my bed in the living room, before completing a consultation with Edna. Bob sat the entire time in his armchair, smoking and making offensive comments about the length of my legs. After he left the room to linger in the hallway, it came time for Edna to undress and she turned to me and said something that makes me laugh to this day.

'Before we start,' she said, 'can I just let you know that Bob has always liked to bugger me quite hard, so it might be a bit of a mess back there.'

'Yes, I have,' Bob shouted through the door.

Even I, with my self-diagnosed Tourette's, was speechless at this truth bomb Edna dropped like she was talking about the weather. And I can confirm that Edna's gutter was indeed just as burst and leaking as the ones at the front of her house.

There was something quite disconcerting about cleaning a pensioner's backside, as her lecherous husband made comments from the next room, but it was a baptism of fire that would stand me in good stead for what lay ahead.

I waxed Edna regularly for three years until she sadly died, At least now her bum rests in peace from the pounding of Bob's hammer – and yes, he did refer to his penis as 'Bob's hammer'. I always imagined it to be nothing like Thor's.

If you are in the slightest bit offended by the love story of Edna and Bob, then it may be time for us to part ways. Consider them an amuse-bouche; a taster of the weird world I inhabit daily.

However, if the vivid image of an obese pensioner, sodomising his partner into oblivion piques your interest, then strap in and join me on a wonderfully bizarre journey. I can't promise you spiritual enrichment or emotional growth but instead, I will tell you all the embarrassing things about my husband that I vowed not to include.

Chapter Three

Grace

A fall from...

As my client base grew, it became clear I needed a treatment room of my own. I considered premises, perhaps a high street shop with glossy signage, fresh and clean inside, white walls, polished floors and a fancy reception desk. Lots of people walking by, lots of hairy vaginas walking past the big windows, all looking to get waxed. I got as far as viewing a few empty shops: an old hairdressing salon, an abandoned sweet shop – jars of lemon sherbets and mint humbugs still on the shelves, and a cobbler's that smelled of leather and glue.

Something niggled at me, though. I have always been a practical thinker, and the more I investigated the cost of having a shop, the more I thought it was a bad idea. Hubby is a self-employed bookkeeper, so he helped me crunch the numbers. I love him, but honestly, I think this was the only time in over a decade together, that I was even slightly interested in anything to do with his work. I don't want you to think badly of me, but this is a man who took a fortnight to decide which model of new calculator he was going to buy. It was during this number crunching that the lightning bolt struck us. Hubby already worked from home most of the time, and all my clients were local, so what could be better than a treatment room/office at the bottom of the garden?

Hubby did all the drawings for the project, as it appealed to him on two fronts. The first, he got to use a ruler, his favourite item of stationery (he admires its precision; yes, he is that boring. He tried talking dirty to me once, comparing his penis to a 9H pencil, the hardest of them all. All I can say is his pencil got nowhere near my sharpener that night). The second, was he got to use a set square, which according to him, is like a ruler on steroids.

After several quotes from local builders it became apparent we couldn't afford any of them. So hubby – with no building experience whatsoever – decided he would undertake the work himself. It worried me. Mostly because I didn't want him to get hurt in the process, but also because I worried about the appearance of the finished product. Still, I won't bore you with the details of the build but the boy did good. I had my treatment room with waiting area, he had his office, and he did it all apart from the electrical work.

It was only after the build was finished I learned the real reason he had been so keen to do it himself. One of the joiners who came out to quote had mentioned how a good workman always measures twice and cuts once. Well, that was hubby sold. Not only did he measure everything twice, but he used two separate tape measures, just in case one was out. Although he did do good, I feel obliged to tell you that the build took two years, instead of the planned six months. Even allowing for measuring everything twice, this was a ridiculous length of time and was purely down to his procrastination. I told him I wouldn't put this bit in the book, but I'm still bloody annoyed as I had to give up my dining room to use as a treatment room in the interim. Hubby was lucky he didn't end up sleeping in the outbuilding.

Anyway, I've got my white walls and polished floors without the need for a fancy reception desk. My treatment room is bright and welcoming and is deliberately on the small side; a TV property show would describe it as bijou. This is not due to a lack of space, but to help make the client feel less vulnerable, and most of the time it works well.

Except when my client Grace comes for an appointment.

Grace is – and I mean this in the nicest possible way – huge. I am not petite myself; standing at a sliver under six feet tall and weighing in at close to fifteen stone, I am big. I was moaning about my size once to hubby and trying to be helpful he said, 'You are not that big… for a man.'

He wasn't trying to be funny, nor was he trying to be hurtful, he genuinely thought it was a compliment. (You can imagine the kind of Valentine's presents I get. In 2004 it was an orbital sander, after I mentioned the banister could do with a rub down.)

Anyway, Grace dwarfs me, both in height and weight.

Despite being classed as morbidly obese, I would be surprised if you could find a happier person. Her laugh is even bigger than she is, and she finds the funny in everything. She is in every way my kind of girl.

As soon as I met her, I was intrigued; she flew in the face of every stereotype you could imagine about a fat person. The first thing that struck me was her clothes, both the quality and how stylish they were. Every cut and stitch of her garments were done by hand and were bespoke. Then there was her jewellery. I am as far from a girly girl as you can get, and the only jewellery I wear are my wedding and engagement rings. Grace is shimmering with jewels – over £20,000 worth on her hands alone, I was soon to learn. To my shame, I immediately assumed she had inherited her money, thinking her too fat to work and too large to be married to a successful partner.

The first lesson Grace taught me was to not judge a book by its cover. She was single. Happily single. And the only child of a working-class couple, so no inheritance. The source of Grace's income is far more spectacular.

Grace is a professional squasher: an obese woman who is paid to sit on men and squash them. There is no sex involved and both parties never have anything less than their underwear on. I had to Google it, as I was sure she was pulling my leg. I now know that it is indeed real – and is one of the many reasons I am so confused as to how men still rule the world. Not to sound sexist, but no woman I know would pay a fat man to sit on their chest.

You won't find Grace anywhere on the internet and she repeatedly refuses to do webcam shows. She gets irritated by those that do, referring to them as 'fame hungry, fat fucks'. I nearly gave myself a hernia laughing when she told me that the only thing those fat bitches were hungrier for than cake, was fame. Grace is strictly by appointment only and she has a very select clientele. I have never encountered anyone who goes to such lengths to protect their client's anonymity. This, she tells me, is because of how much they stand to lose. All are millionaires several times over and most are very successful, powerful men. I suppose, anyone with even the most basic grasp of psychology, could quickly make the link between these men and their jobs, and how out of control they are when being squashed.

Whatever their reason for frequenting Grace, they pay very well. Not only do they pay her fee, they also regularly give her lavish gifts, hence the jewellery.

You can imagine, though, that being so large does come with problems, and one of them is the logistics of an intimate wax. Grace has, what she calls a 'four hander' for an arse – that it would take four hands to pull her butt cheeks apart far enough to get to her anus. I only have two hands so that makes waxing her butt particularly tricky. If you have never had an intimate wax, you may not be aware that the easiest way to wax a butt is to get the client up on all fours. This is not the demurest of positions, but it is the most efficient.

It was at this point during one of Grace's waxes, that I witnessed something so funny I wet my pants. I literally laughed so hard I wet myself.

Grace was on the bed on all fours and I had my back to her while at my wax pot. I turned around just as Sir Mix-A-Lot's *Baby Got Back (I Like Big Butts)* came on the stereo. Had it been anyone else I might have put the music off, but I knew it was one of Grace's favourite songs. And for a moment, as the beat started, Grace forgot where she was and started to sway her hips in rhythm. I have never seen anything like it, as she swayed from side to side her folds of flesh took a couple of seconds to catch up with her skeleton. It was happening as if in slow motion and I swear it was hypnotic. I was mesmerised.

Then catastrophe, Grace's left arm buckled under her weight and as the momentum of her hip gathered, she threw herself off the bed, landing on her back with a thud. It took me a moment to register what had happened as my head was still moving in time with the meaty metronome. We both started to laugh. I don't know if you have ever seen a 400-pound woman, naked from the waist down, throw herself from a bed in time with a Sir-Mix-A-Lot classic, but I have – and I wet myself.

It quickly became clear that we had a problem. Grace had fallen between the bed and the wall and she didn't have the strength in her stomach muscles to sit up. There was no room at either her head or feet for me to get in and help her. I know what you are thinking: why not just move the bed? Well, I had made the mistake, a few weeks before, of mentioning to Captain Ruler that my bed wasn't stable when clients were climbing onto it. He promptly got out his tool box and bolted the bed to the floor. And now he wasn't home, and Grace was squashed. The irony wasn't wasted on her.

I tried to make her comfortable whilst we waited for hubby to return and unbolt the bed. Doing my best to protect her modesty, I covered her bottom half with a towel, and I popped a pillow under her head. We filled the time by talking about our favourite foods, something we regularly do during her appointments. I always end up famished after Grace's wax.

So, when my husband arrived home, he walked in to see a beautiful, big woman, flat on her back, naked from the waist down, excitedly talking about the best burger she'd ever had.

Most people would have been surprised, but not him. He was too bloody busy congratulating himself on what a good job he had done fitting the bolts.

I left the two of them to go and change my trousers, and when I came back Grace was picking hubby's brain about whether she could claim all her food as a business expense.

I finished the wax with Grace on the floor, and some Lynyrd Skynyrd on the stereo.

CHAPTER FOUR

Stewart

MASSIVE COCK UP...

Once I was satisfied I had perfected the female intimate wax, I began thinking about the male intimate wax – a completely different beast.

Of course, you use the same wax for both, and yes, when it comes to butts, we are all pretty much working with the same equipment. Around the front, though... Well, unless you were born in a convent, I am pretty sure you know the difference.

Logistics aside, there is another difference, and that is psychology.

Men and women think very differently, especially when it comes to sex. We all think about sex, women just as much as men, despite the common misconception to the contrary, but the problem men tend to have is the way they think about it. Most guys grow up watching porn films, where a seemingly mundane situation turns into a wild sex orgy. The pizza guy is at the door – and minutes later he's in the busty blonde's pants. The plumber comes to fix the leak under the sink – and before you know it the foxy brunette is adjusting his spanner. You know the kind of thing.

The male brain becomes conditioned to believe that in a situation where someone happens to be looking at his penis, there is every chance that that someone might pop said penis in their mouth. An intimate wax fits squarely into this type of scenario. When women book in for an intimate wax, they normally only think about the wax itself, or how happy they will be with the result. When (some) men book in, a part of their brain automatically goes to a 'happy ending'.

So, the first male brain I had to think of was my husband's. I am a strong, independent woman and I didn't need my husband's blessing to wax men, but I wanted it. Having been together for years, I knew there was no chance he would try to dissuade me from waxing willies but for my own piece of mind, I needed to speak to him before signing up for the additional training courses.

Waiting until the kids were in bed one night, I decided to broach the subject. It led to a massive argument. Not because he tried to put his foot down and stamp his authority. Not because he didn't want his wife touching another man's cock.

But because he wasn't in the slightest bit bothered about his wife touching another man's cock.

I took this as a massive insult. I took it to mean that he thought no man would want to do anything to me with their cock. Over the hill, two kids down, and no sex appeal, was what I heard him say. Who the hell did he think he was? The smug bastard. Did he think he was improving with age, and providing a service by staying with someone so grotesque?

Of course, he didn't say any of those things. That all took place in my head. He said the reason it didn't bother him was that he loved me, and he knew I loved him. That we had two beautiful kids and a life together. So, why would he be in the least bit insecure about me waxing men?

It turns out I married one of the few men that hadn't seen any porn films where the driving instructor accidentally makes the student use the wrong gear stick. With his love of numbers, he probably grew up masturbating to Carol Vorderman on Countdown. I later asked him about this and he told me he did try, but he lost his erection every time Richard Whitely appeared on screen.

With the green light from hubby, I booked my additional training, which went smoothly. To get my certificate, I just needed to bring a model for my final assessment. That wasn't quite as easy. Most men tend to get very nervous about exposing themselves in such a situation. Hubby ruled himself out as soon as he realised that it wasn't just me and the assessor in the room. There would be multiple beds set out, with several waxers doing their exam. Oddly, he wasn't bothered about getting his tackle out, the problem was he didn't want his arse on display whilst on all fours. I reminded him of this the next time he wanted to take me from behind.

I didn't have many other options. Most of the men I knew were dads from the school, and I didn't want to be known as the mum that stands at the school gates asking to wax guys cocks. I can't imagine the kids would get invited to too many birthday parties after that. Or maybe they would get invited to more, who knows?

I was fortunate enough to have one guy in my life, who had absolutely no problem in putting his arse in the air – my fabulously gay friend Stewart. He agreed to come and be my model.

Stewart is wonderful, and the only real connection left to the wild days of my youth, when I was single, with no kids, and no responsibilities, other than a crappy job. Like most people, I sometimes fantasise about those days and miss the footloose, carefree me. Then I look at my family and don't regret a thing.

On the day of the assessment it dawned on me, that despite all the years I have known Stewart, I had never seen his cock. Once we were set up, with Stewart laid on his back, a towel covering his middle, the assessor came to my station and asked me to begin. As I pulled the towel back, I revealed something which, I could only assume, was meant to be attached to a horse. I had never seen anything like it before or since, not on a human anyway. Mary, the assessor, not able to contain herself uttered, 'Jesus Christ', which she repeatedly apologised for.

It was a real test, of not only my waxing abilities, but strength; my arms burned with the effort of moving the colossus about.

The real stand out moment, though, was when Stewart positioned himself on all-fours, and Mary and I were confronted with what looked like a mouse's tail coming from his butthole. Memories of an urban legend from the nineties about Richard Gere came flooding back to me. The story went that Mr Gere, for sexual gratification, inserted a gerbil into his anus. Unable to retrieve the rodent, he then had to attend hospital to have it surgically removed. This is, of course, pure nonsense, but it has followed him like a bad smell for decades. And just when he thinks it has disappeared, here comes a fanny waxer to remind everyone about it.

It is funny how things resonate with you, though, as for a split second I genuinely thought Stewart had shoved a mouse up his arse. Images of Mickey Mouse singing his TV theme tune, invaded my brain. Please no, don't ruin Disney for me, Stewart, I thought.

It turned out that his other half, just as well-endowed as him, is, shall we say, the giver in the relationship. Stewart always prefers to receive, whether it is Christmas gifts or birthday presents. Or massive penises, it would seem. Yes, he had suffered the same fate as Edna. A burst gutter. I wondered if he had encountered Bob and his hammer. Anyway, to prevent any possible leakage, Stewart had popped a tampon up his bum.

'Erm, Stewart... ' Before I could finish the sentence, he said,

'Oh shit. I've left a tampon in, haven't I?'

And before we could even step away to give him some privacy he reached around and pulled it out.

I heard Mary gag a little and hoped that I didn't get marked down. If anything, she was very impressed with the cool and calm way I dealt with the matter; she said she had never encountered anything like it in her career. Clearly, she'd been fortunate, as I had seen far worse already. I was just happy that my image of Mickey remained intact.

Hubby had expected there wouldn't be much of a market for male waxing, particularly where we lived in the suburbs of a mid-sized town. I think he had the stereotypical image of a male wax client, either gay or metrosexual. To give you an idea of how archaic his thought processes are, metrosexual, a term coined in 1994, is his most up-to-date reference point for a well groomed man. This is particularly offensive, given that his own pubic hair is so long it has formed into ringlets, nestling either side of his penis and giving it the appearance of a Yemenite Jew.

As it turned out, he couldn't have been more wrong. At the time of writing, male clients account for almost thirty five percent of my workload. And yes, some of them are gay and some of them are well-groomed. By and large, though, most of them are what hubby would call 'normal blokes'. I would like to clarify that he doesn't find anything abnormal about being gay or well-groomed, by normal he means guys like him. Men who outwardly appear to have given up somewhat – hair a little messy, unkempt stubble, and clothes purchased from a supermarket. Basically, he thinks anyone who is a middle-aged dad is a normal bloke.

My male clients come from all walks of life. Amongst my clientele I have truck drivers, surfers, doctors, students, footballers, bin men (or waste collection operatives, which I am told is their pc job title), lawyers, and so on. Age is no barrier either, my youngest client being eighteen and my oldest eighty-two. Some are thin, some are fat, and some are chiselled hunks of muscle. Hubby assures me that all of those are certainly gay. As is Alexander Skarsgård, apparently, but only since we saw him in Tarzan and I commented on his torso.

The one thing my male clients all have in common is the fear of an unwanted erection, something all men experience at some point in their lives. Whether it is as a teenager standing at the front of the class to do a presentation, with a bulge in the trousers, or sitting on a bus and having to miss their stop because they have pitched a tent whilst the bus has motored along. Even at the doctor's surgery for a testicular examination with a throbbing hard-on. These scenarios do happen and more regularly than you may imagine.

Apparently, thinking hard about not getting an erection has the opposite effect – as if the penis cannot distinguish between its own on and off switch; it merely knows that the brain is thinking about the switch and assumes it must be getting flicked to on. Not dissimilar to a dog that thinks it's going out for a walk: the dog simply thinks somebody has mentioned the word walk and it is jumping for joy. Neither will give up easily and both will keep jumping up for attention.

The fear of an uninvited stiffy obviously plays a big part in getting waxed. As part of the treatment I obviously need to touch the penis. This alone is enough for some men to get hard, and I know it can be a source of embarrassment as most guys don't want to be perceived as a sex pest. Don't get me wrong, that little voice is still in the background for some guys, chanting, 'happy ending, happy ending', but they wouldn't dare say it. Most people don't want to come across as a pervert.

In order to allay their fears, I have a conversation with every new client. I assure them that getting an erection is a perfectly normal response during the treatment, and it won't be taken as a sexual advance. I am perfectly clear, though, that this is purely a professional service, and should there be any inappropriate behaviour then hot wax will be poured on the head of their penis. Good luck removing that.

Only once, have I been made to feel truly uncomfortable by a male client, an incident that left me uneasy, to say the least. It was the client's first time with me, and nothing so far had struck me as strange. We went through the consultation process and I stepped out of the room to allow him to get undressed and positioned on the bed. It was once I started to apply the wax that things got strange.

'Do you know who this treatment would be good for?' he asked as I was waiting for the applied wax to harden.

'Who's that?' I replied.

'A rapist,' he said.

'Sorry?' I was startled.

'Well, it removes the hair from the root, so there is no DNA evidence,' he said as if it was the most normal thing in the world.

I quickly removed the wax and explained I was ending the treatment there. I never ask clients to undress or dress in front of me, I always leave the room to give them some privacy. But this guy, I made dress in front of me and then I chucked him out. I reported him to the police who later informed me that the address and contact details he had supplied on his consultation form were fake. I shudder to think what would have happened had he come across someone who didn't have my balls.

Chapter Five

Cynthia

The black and blues...

If male intimate waxing can prove difficult for a lot of beauticians, in all honesty female intimate waxing isn't much easier. Lots of girls get into beauty as they love beautiful things: sparkly fake nails, spray tans, glossy hairdos and full-face make-up. All very pretty.

Hairy fannies and balls, not so much. I know beauticians who make a face like they are changing a shitty nappy every time they carry out an intimate wax. Can you imagine how degrading that is for a client? Exposing yourself in all your glory, only for your waxer to make a face like they are cleaning dog crap off a shoe.

I have never had that problem. I am not a beautician, I am a waxer, and I didn't get into my job because I like sparkly things. I am not a typical girl, which is largely down to my upbringing.

The purpose of this book is to try and make you laugh, which I hope it does. But to give you an idea of why I am not a typical girl, I need to explain to you the pretty bleak affair that was my childhood.

In short, my father was an unemployed bum and violent alcoholic who beat his wife and four daughters. As the oldest I served as a surrogate son and as the gobbiest, it was me who received most of his wrath. That said, I don't want you to think that it defines me in any way, other than making me as strong as I am today.

Anyway, that's a whole different book. My point is I didn't get to be sparkly and pink and girly, I got to live in the shadows and be black and blue. But I promise you something: I made sure to find the funny in it. So, whenever I came home and found my father passed out naked on the stairs, covered in his own vomit, I laughed. Even as a child I knew how pathetic and laughable he was. And I appreciated every morsel of humour I could get, as laughter was a rare commodity in our house.

My experiences growing up taught me to strive for a better life. I have always worked very hard as I didn't want to be a deadbeat like my father. My first job was at thirteen, which coincidentally, happened to be the same time I started paying dig money. I also provided extra food and sanitary products for my sisters, as my parents wouldn't. Whilst my friends were lying in bed on a Saturday morning I had been at work for hours. So, I would never turn my nose up at any client during an intimate wax. I appreciate every client I have or have ever had. I know what it's like to have nothing, something which I am proud to say, my kids don't.

A combination of my personality, and my less than perfect upbringing, have made me particularly good at dealing with male clients. My ability to talk to them about 'blokey' things like boxing and football makes me less intimidating than most female waxers. Bad language was also a staple of my childhood, so I can exchange curse words with the best of them. Plus, after watching your father stumble about pissed and naked most Friday nights, a half-naked man on your treatment bed is a walk in the park.

Although a big personality forged in a rough upbringing can certainly come in handy when you are an intimate waxer, my approach isn't always well received, and I am somewhat of an anomaly in the town that I now live. Hubby and I met at work, many years ago in my hometown. He was the fish out of water there. In his hometown, where we currently stay, people don't get mugged for their trainers, which was a regular occurrence where I grew up.

Admittedly, my tastes may have become a little more sophisticated as I have got older, but my personality has remained the same. This doesn't sit too well with some of the ladies who lunch, and they would much rather that I just conform.

Usually, I can ignore the snide comments and accept that some people need to feel superior to get by. Cynthia, though, one of my snootier clients, did manage to get under my skin.

Ordinarily, I don't think you should ever base your opinion of someone on their appearance, unless they're dressed as a nun, but that's mainly down to six years of Catholic secondary schooling, where most of the nuns made my father look like a saint (we weren't religious, the Catholic school was just three miles closer than the non-denomination secondary). However, Cynthia has chosen to ape anti-style icon and morally bankrupt wind-bag Margaret Thatcher. Think tailored skirt-suits, pussybow blouses and pearl necklaces, the timeless look for the woman about town looking to close mines and steal milk from children. She keeps the suit jacket on during her wax, which never fails to unnerve me; imagine waxing a half-dressed Maggie's fanny. Terrifying.

You may imagine that Cynthia has a high-flying career in the city, something in finance, perhaps? But you would be wrong. She is a twenty-something stay-at-home mum. So, why the power dressing? In truth nobody knows. And people have asked. Because you might not get mugged for your trainers in this town, but the gossips will make off with your life-story like a deft-fingered pickpocket at the Piazza Navona in Rome. All I can tell you is that she didn't always identify as a right-wing clothes horse.

Other clients, who knew Cynthia growing up, remember her as a denims, t-shirt, and trainers kinda girl, who drank cider straight out of the bottle, up the local swing park. And let me tell you, the things I've heard she did with boys under the slide would have caught her more than harsh looks from the Sisters of No Mercy at my school – the vicious little penguins (I had a chalk duster thrown off my face just for saying I didn't believe in god. Thanks Sister McGonigle).

The Cynthia I know has been afflicted with a desire to see people doing badly. It is not good enough for her to be doing well, she needs people to be suffering – she may be missing her real calling within the Catholic church. I'm sure you've met a Cynthia at some point in your life, and I'm equally sure you thought she was an arsehole.

A usual appointment with Cynthia is peppered with bragging mixed with gossiping. All on her part, I would add, I rarely open my mouth. Once she starts, she barely stops to breathe. Among her favourite topics are how successful her husband is and how much money he makes. Suffice to say, she did not meet him up the swing park and it is highly unlikely he knows about her under-the-slide dalliances. Despite her telling me multiple times what he does I can never remember, it's something to do with network planning. What kind of network I don't know, and I would rather gargle diesel than ask her.

Normally I take everything in my stride, but it was as Cynthia was leaving one day that I took the bait. As I was seeing her out, she noticed my new car sat on the driveway. Now, in all the years hubby and I had been together we had never really bought ourselves anything nice. All our money went on the kids and bills. But I had been working extra hard and for the first time ever I bought myself a nice car. Some may see it as an indulgence, but I felt I had earned it.

Cynthia was furious because it was nicer than hers – not something I noticed, but she clearly had. What she said floored me.

'You're originally from a council estate in a really poor area, are you not?' she asked indignantly, fingering her pearl necklace.

'Yes. So?' I asked.

'Well, haven't you done well for yourself,' she said as patronisingly as she could. 'And all from waxing?'

Hubby has never quite forgiven me for what I said next and he is still waiting for a knock on the door.

'Oh, not just waxing,' I replied. 'I'm also a drug dealer. As a matter of fact, I'm your girl if you're looking for any coke this weekend.'

Probably not wise to tell one of the biggest town gossips that you are a drug dealer, but it was worth it to see the look on her face, even if it could have led to the boys in blue swooping in for a drug bust.

Chapter Six

Sarah

A case of mistaken identity...

Although I may seem a little uncouth to many of the well-to-do ladies of the town, I am nothing compared to my client and friend Debbie.

Deb's upbringing mirrored mine, brought up in a council estate in a poor town blighted by unemployment. The main difference between us was fathers, mine was an arsehole and hers was absent. Deb was raised by her mum who was a formidable character and often a questionable role model. By the age of fourteen she had seen sights many will never see. Her family home was like a drop-in centre for losers: alcoholics and drug addicts coming and going, thieves fencing stolen goods, and the kind of guys you never want around young girls. If anything, she had it much worse than me, as I only had to deal with one shit of a human being, she had dozens of them every week.

An upbringing like this tends to do one of two things to people. It either breaks you and you spend the rest of your life being a victim, or it galvanises your spirit and makes you stronger. With Deb it was the latter. After marrying a man with both an equally troubled background, and as strong a spirit as her, they have built a massively successful business from nothing. She now lives in one of the most desirable streets in town, her neighbours being a mix of old and new money – who are all in agreement that she is not their kind of person. Deb is more than aware of their disdain for her and she thrives on it.

Deb is the very definition of an over sharer; her entire life is an open book. In her own inimitable style, she regularly posts her appointments with me on Facebook. Her most recent post was: *Thank fuck I've got my wax today, my fanny looks like a young Michael Jackson, but it's produced more number ones!*

I feel very fortunate to have Deb as a friend, as she is a constant reminder to keep true to myself, there are too many fake people nowadays, who like to forget where they came from. Yes, she swears a lot. Yes, she has no social awareness. And yes, she will call bullshit whenever she hears it, regardless of where she might be. But she is honest, warm, loyal, and fiercely protective of those she loves, and in my opinion these traits are far more desirable in a person than civility.

Deb has three wonderful kids, who have benefited from the kind of childhood she missed out on. A loving family home with supportive parents, plenty of food in the kitchen and toys galore. I am particularly fond of her youngest daughter, Claire, who is an absolute angel. Deb often brought her along to her appointments when she was little, where she would sit in the waiting room and watch Peppa Pig. I made a big fuss of her every visit; at nearly ten years younger than my youngest, it was nice to spend time with a tiny tot again.

One beautiful summer morning, I was in my workroom updating my diary, and waiting for Deb to arrive for her wax. I heard the pitter patter of little feet outside in the waiting room and peered round the door to see little Claire, her back to me, dressed in a beautiful pink summer dress, staring out the window at the kids playing in the garden. I tiptoed towards her as quietly as I could and scooped her up in my arms, and began to spin her round and round. 'Weeeeeeeee!' I shrieked, as I went faster and faster.

Claire struggled to break free from my grip, so I tickled her to make her laugh. Usually she was such a happy child with the most infectious giggle. Today, though, she seemed tense and I wondered if there was something wrong. As we spun, I looked to the door for Deb; it was strange she had not come in yet.

Unbeknown to me, Deb had left a voicemail cancelling her appointment, which I would not discover until later that day.

'Will you fucking put me down!' Claire said angrily.

Except it wasn't Claire, it was my new client, Sarah, who was due in at ten but had turned up early. You see Sarah is a dwarf. Yep, I had picked up a twenty-seven-year-old woman and spun her round my waiting room shouting, 'Weeeeeeeee', and then tickled her for good measure.

Sarah was exceptionally pissed off. She didn't know I was waiting for my friend to come in with her young daughter. To her, she had just been manhandled by a stranger. I wished the ground could have opened and swallowed me. I'm very rarely stuck for words, but for what seemed like forever, I couldn't get anything out of my mouth. Then eventually the best I could manage was, 'I thought you were a child', which served only to piss her off even more. I somehow pulled myself together and was able to explain my behaviour.

Sarah seemed satisfied.

'Oh good, I'm so glad we got that sorted,' I said, before doing something that I have absolutely no explanation for, and which the thought of makes me shudder to this day. After having my apology accepted, I patted her on the head. *What the fuck was going through my mind?* Not only did I pat her on the head, but I realised I shouldn't have been doing it, and mid-pat I stopped and just rested my hand on her head, before ruffling her hair.

Fortunately, Sarah was a little more composed than me and she told me to take a few deep breaths and start again.

After a rocky start, Sarah and I got on famously. We had more in common than you would initially think. We both had been victims of bullying at school because of our height. Sarah obviously because she was short, and me because I was freakishly tall for a girl. Most high street chains now have a tall section, but back in the day, I either had to wear boys' clothes or look like my school uniform had shrunk in the wash. If I'm honest it wasn't as if I had much of an option anyway, as my deadbeat dad used my clothing grant money from school to buy booze. This meant my sisters and I had to wear hand-me-downs from our older cousins, who were all boys.

We both had a love for travel, too. Sarah is not from the UK, and was here as part of a year out, travelling. We compared places we had been and discussed places we would love to go.

Although Sarah was only a one-time client, I learned a lot from her and I wish she had stayed around for longer; I would love to have gone out for drinks with her. She taught me to look at the world from a different perspective. I haven't always enjoyed being tall, and although it is usually seen as an advantage, it didn't seem like that as a gangly teenager, when I just wanted to be invisible. Self-consciousness aside, I have never suffered any of the difficulties that Sarah has. Simple things like using public toilets, getting up on hotel beds, shopping in the supermarket, that I take for granted, are challenges for Sarah. Everything I can do with ease is so much harder for her. On top of that her height continues to be a source of ridicule, whereas mine now, is barely noteworthy. People, she told me, think that it is okay to take photos of her as she is going about her day-to-day life.

Despite the ignorance of others, she, like me, loves to find the funny in everything. Her height doesn't define her, her personality does. One of her favourite things is to go to the cinema to watch a horror film, and just as it is getting to a scary bit, she sneaks out of her seat and stands silently at the end of a row to scare the shit out of people. She told me it works particularly well with a film like Orphan, where the source of terror is a child. She even goes as far to put her hair in pigtails to complete the look.

On her travels she was compiling a list of which nationalities made the best lovers. It wasn't an official research project or anything she told me, winking, just purely for fun. It turns out the Brits rated quite highly, hence the wax, as she had a hot date that night.

I was glad when she brought up the list of lovers, as it was a subject that I wanted to broach but couldn't. Regardless of how well we were getting along, I had to remain professional, and talking about a client's sex life isn't something I would bring up first. Sarah could clearly sense my curiosity, though, and she answered the question before I even asked it.

'Yes, I get some weirdoes,' she explained, 'but I'm pretty good at weeding them out before it gets too serious.'

She went on to explain how it was usually easy to spot the guys that wanted her to dress up to satisfy their predilection for young girls. It was just another difficulty in life she had to overcome.

Although Sarah had honed her ability to spot an oddball over the years, she told me how she was caught off guard by a guy that she had dated for four months.

Everything seemed perfectly normal at first: Ethan was just her type, six feet two inches tall, clean cut and muscular. He was an absolute gentleman, who paid when they went on dates; polite and courteous always. He had a good job, his own home, a strong group of friends, and a wonderful family. To top it off the sex was fantastic, in her top three. It all seemed too good to be true, and for four months it was perfect. And that's when it unravelled. After returning home from a night out, things were getting steamy, and Ethan brought up the subject of fantasies. Sarah told me that she was very vanilla and just liked good old-fashioned sex, so she didn't have much to share with him. Ethan on the other hand, had a doozy.

Apparently, he had kept a secret for years, never telling anyone that nothing made him harder than the thought of being a giant. He even had a costume hidden in a case at the back of his wardrobe – one modelled on the giant from Jack and the Beanstalk. It was at this point Sarah realised that Ethan had orchestrated a four-month relationship with her, because her height would allow him to act out his long-held fairy-tale fantasy.

Fee-fi-fo-fum, Ethan's going to destroy your bum.

I don't know if he was a fan of anal sex, but that's the line that kept running through my head.

In lieu of a beanstalk, Sarah escaped down the stairs and that was the last time she ever saw Ethan. Although he was perfect in every other way, she said that the relationship could never work, it would always be based on her height and not true love. I admire her for that, not all women value themselves enough to hold out for Mr Right. I have plenty of single friends who would happily wank off a guy dressed as the BFG, if he had his own place and a job.

All told, Sarah was only in my life for a little under an hour, but she made an impact that will last a lifetime. I have always tried to instil a thirst for knowledge in my children, not only from school, but also from every person that they meet in life. I believe that you can learn something from everyone. Sarah taught me that we are all responsible for our own sense of self-worth. Because of her height, many people would think she should be grateful for any shot at love that she gets. They certainly wouldn't think she should be picky. But Sarah knows her true sense of worth and it shines from her.

Chapter Seven

Paul

Oopsie...

This next story, technically, has nothing to do with waxing, and is more an outcome of where I wax from. Plus, it is a great example of how humour can be found in the direst of circumstances, so I have to include it.

We are very fortunate to be able to work from home. No rush hour traffic with roads tailed back for miles. No trains rammed with commuters, standing room only. And best of all, absolutely no travel expenses.

There are other concerns, however, particularly when you have clients coming to you and they need to park in your street. As we live in a quiet suburban area, and most of our neighbours are retired, this could have been a major problem. Fortunately, there are some benefits to being married to a man who has almost all the same interests as a pensioner. I couldn't even begin to guess how much time hubby has spent out the front of our house, sharing stories with men old enough to be his grandfather. It's like an episode of Last of the Summer Wine, in which the casting director screwed up one of the roles. So, any time one of our clients parks too close to a neighbour's drive, and they get a little frustrated, I just send Compo out to smooth things over.

It helps that hubby is genuinely a nice guy, who can regularly be found doing odd jobs for the older neighbours. This includes, but is not limited to climbing on to rooftops to replace broken tiles and cutting down trees – which nearly cost him his right hand in a chainsaw-related accident, running rubbish to the local dump. One neighbour, prompted by a sudden interest in Feng Shui, is particularly fond of getting him to help move furniture around the house. At the ripe old age of eighty-two, I fail to see how moving his sideboard from one wall to the other will massively affect his health, wealth, and happiness, but what do I know? Hubby is always happy to help, though, and it certainly doesn't do any harm to bank a little goodwill from the people you live next to.

While it wasn't abnormal for our furniture-bothering neighbour to be ringing our doorbell to ask for assistance, calling early on a Saturday morning was a little out of the ordinary. As he repeatedly rang the bell at 7.50am, I must admit that I was a little peeved at his thoughtlessness. Although we were both up – hubby to deal with the kids, and me for my first client at 8.30am – I thought to myself, really Keith, just how badly do you need to move your chaise longue from the hallway?

As it turned out, Keith's visit was a little more urgent than a reshuffle of his wicker chairs in the sun room. Keith and his wife, like many of our retired neighbours, are early morning gardeners. I think this is an anomaly largely reserved for the elderly, where the need for sleep and the need to potter become inversely proportional as you reach a certain age. I hope you do not think I am being ageist, but if you look at the various age groups of society, almost all of them would love a lie-in on a Saturday morning. Kids under twelve may be the exception to the rule, as any parent knows. Most kids given the opportunity to deprive their parents of an extra hour in bed will do so gleefully. If you don't have kids, ask someone that does, then look at the sadness in their eyes, as they try to remember the last opportunity they had for a lie-in. Teenagers are a different story altogether, trying to waken a fourteen-year-old for school is like trying to push a reluctant elephant up a steep hill. When adolescents are between the ages of thirteen and nineteen, broken and exhausted parents reap revenge for all the lie-ins stolen from them, by the very people they gave life to. Nothing excites a beleaguered parent more than getting to ruin a teenagers lie-in. This is petty I agree, but when you dedicate pretty much two solid decades of your life to a generally unappreciative audience, you need to take the small wins where you can get them.

Young adults in their twenties lie-in on a Saturday, trying to stave off the after effects of the night before. With nothing to get up for, the weekend their own, they will happily lie-in till noon. As you go up through the ages, into the thirties and forties, and further to the fifties, most people would relish the thought of a lie-in, just to try and make a dent in the perpetual exhaustion caused by our manic modern lifestyles. But pensioners are a law unto themselves. The one time in our life since childhood where we can lie-in as often as we want, and our bodies betray us. My father-in-law is a prime example, he can't sleep past 3a.m. As a matter of fact, he received complaints from his neighbours, as he began regularly cutting his grass at 5a.m. He was dumbfounded by their reaction, as to him it was mid-morning.

I have digressed somewhat I am afraid, one of my more frustrating character traits, according to hubby. Anyway, Keith and Sylvie had been in their front garden weeding, when their next-door neighbour Liz had come running out, shouting for help, because her husband had fallen and was stuck. Liz's husband, Paul, was largely housebound due to a serious condition affecting his heart and lungs that meant he was on oxygen twenty-four-hours a day. He was the only neighbour that hubby had never spoken to, despite years of living across the road from each other. This was purely down to Paul's gruff nature, hubby tried to speak to him on various occasions, with no success. Paul wouldn't even return his waves; there is something tragic about watching your grown-up husband pouting, because a stranger won't wave at him.

Anyway, as Paul was a large man, in excess of twenty stone, Keith knew he was going to need help. Hubby is the youngest man in the street by quite a stretch, and at over six feet tall and twenty-plus stone himself, he is also a big guy. So, Keith found himself on our doorstep ringing the doorbell incessantly. When hubby answered he was met with a very panicked octogenarian. All he could say was, 'Paul's in trouble', before fleeing up the path. Well, fleeing may be an exaggeration, Keith is after all in his eighties. 'Shuffled quickly' may be more appropriate.

Hubby hurriedly grabbed a pair of trainers and ran across the road, still in his Darth Vader pyjamas. In his defence, not his choice, they were a Father's Day present, and said in big letters under Darth Vader's helmet, 'I'm your father'. Just to complete the visual image in your head the set consisted of matching pyjama t-shirt and shorts.

Keith led the way into Liz and Paul's house, a small two bed bungalow they had downsized to, once the kids had flown the nest. At the end of the narrow hallway, off to the right was the master bedroom.

Hubby entered to be confronted with Paul on his knees on the floor, his legs crossed at the ankles, body bent forward, arms awkwardly trapped under his torso, and his face buried deep in the shag pile carpet. With a double bed, wardrobes and three sets of drawers, the room was very tight. Paul had been sitting on the edge of the bed just before he keeled over, and now found himself trapped between the bed and the wall. He also found himself wearing only the boxer shorts he slept in.

If you haven't already got the measure of how bizarre my husband is, then let me enlighten you further. It was at this point, in what was clearly an emergency, that he noted Paul was wearing the same pants as him. It concerned him slightly, given the forty-year age gap between them – the only time I have heard him express concern about any of his clothing. And this is a man who for most of the late nineties wore a rubber jacket; apparently rubber was far more practical than leather, which all his friends were wearing.

After getting over the shock of them being pants twins, hubby and Keith attempted to take an arm each and lift Paul, to position him on his back. Unfortunately, as Paul's arms were trapped underneath him they were unable to lift his weight. The problem was compounded by the fact that Keith, at eighty-two-years of age, hadn't been at the gym in a while and didn't have the upper body strength needed for the task.

Since his face had been forced down in the thick carpet, hubby feared Paul was unable to breathe. He decided he was going to have to force his arms under Paul's armpits, link hands behind his back and lift him into a bear hug, all before placing him flat on the floor.

For somebody so fond of mathematics, Hubby made three massive miscalculations. Firstly, he wholly underestimated just how sweaty Paul's body was, something he wouldn't accurately gauge until he had already committed to the lift. Secondly, he underestimated just how heavy Paul was. And thirdly, he massively overestimated his own strength.

These three factors combined, led to a scene worthy of a Three Stooges film. Just as he positioned his arms behind Paul's back, unbeknown to hubby, Liz appeared in the doorway. Hubby heaved with all his might and was able to lift Paul up, until his head was at chest height. At this point his arms slipped against Paul's sweat-slicked skin, and then they gave up on him. And in front of the man's wife, he dropped Paul on his face and as he fell, my husband, who prides himself on his use of the English language, could only find the word, 'Oopsie'. Paul hit the floor with a thud. Rolling slightly as he fell, his face was revealed for the first time, and Liz said, 'It's okay, he has gone.'

As they looked down, it certainly didn't seem promising for Paul, his skin was grey, and his lips were tinged with blue. By this time Keith was on the phone to the emergency services who were instructing him how to do CPR. I think their instructions were somewhat lost in translation however, as it was at this point that I arrived, and it looked like Keith was trying to tickle him.

I am fortunate enough to have completed a Heartstart course at the kids' school, so I immediately took over CPR. I don't know if this is something that you have ever done, but it is not quite as easy as it seems on TV hospital dramas. It is physically exhausting and before long I was spent. (Side note: I was on my period at the time, and the exertion of the compressions forced my tampon out. This attracted one of Liz's King Charles Spaniels who proceeded to muzzle my crotch like a pig hunting for truffles, as I attempted to save his master's life – so much for man's best friend.) At this point I asked hubby to take over. He had not attended the Heartstart course, but I assumed he was watching me and would replicate what I was doing. I went back across the road to check on the kids and, a little overwhelmed with the situation, to start cancelling my clients.

Almost immediately after I left, much to hubby's relief, three paramedics turned up. As they entered the room he automatically stood, to allow them access. One of the paramedics stopped him and asked him to continue performing CPR. This did not appeal to hubby's sense of practicality at all. He was an untrained member of the public providing what was potentially a live saving procedure, whilst three highly trained professionals watched on. It was only after Paul had been hooked up to various bits of machinery, hubby was relieved of his duty and asked to leave the room.

Liz was waiting nervously in the living room with Sylvie, while hubby stood in the hallway. He could tell from the hushed conversation between the paramedics that Paul had passed away long before they arrived. Not only that, he discovered that he hadn't been performing CPR properly, as he had been bending his elbows rather than keeping them locked. He realised immediately the paramedics would have noticed that as soon as they came in, but they allowed him to continue without comment.

He moaned to me later, 'So, they effectively let me massage a corpse for ten minutes whilst they watched.'

I became slightly concerned about his mental state after this incident, because he went straight to work that morning. I was so shattered I cancelled my entire day. The following week, during an unrelated appointment with my GP, I was discussing hubby's reaction to the situation, and the doctor suggested that if he wasn't affected, I might be married to a psychopath. Later, I realised he simply uses humour to deal with dark situations, something he has done since he was a young child.

It turned out that Paul's kids did the same thing. His two sons, both in their forties, had come round to sit with their mum while the funeral director visited. He was a serious man in his mid-fifties and had brought along a lad in his late teens, who was serving his apprenticeship at the funeral parlour. After making the various arrangements for the service, the funeral director asked if the family had considered putting an intimation in the local paper. Paul's eldest son replied, 'We'll probably just do what everyone in this town does when there is an event like a birthday or an anniversary. We'll hang a bed sheet from the bridge and write on it in paint, 'DADDY'S DEAD CARAVAN FOR SALE'.

The funeral director, by all accounts, was not impressed, the apprentice however, laughed until he cried.

Paul's funeral was a real eye opener. It was the first occasion we had reason to spend any amount of time with all our neighbours together. Sure, we had been round for a barbecue with the people next door a couple of times, and occasionally someone might pop in for a drink at Christmas. But in all the years living in the street, that was about the extent of it. From the get-go it was clear the funeral was going to be eventful.

Paul and Liz lived to one side of Keith and Sylvie, and on the other side were Ben and Lynne. At the end of the street was our oldest resident, Sammy, who at 92 was old enough to have served as a Paratrooper in World War Two.

Sammy set the tone for the day almost immediately. Having been a widower for over two decades, he lacked the direction his wife used to provide. He appeared on Ben and Lynne's doorstep, ready for a lift to the crematorium, wearing a natty blue and gold Hawaiian shirt and a pair of well-worn tennis shoes alongside his suit. Sammy explained he had misplaced his white dress shirt and black shoes and, bizarrely, rather than select another solid coloured shirt from his wardrobe, he chose the ensemble of a rather dishevelled Don Johnson from Miami Vice. If you are too young to remember Don Johnson, or indeed Miami Vice, then ask your mum. Or possibly your gran.

Due to a lack of time, and the fact that Ben and Lynne are both in their mid-eighties and barely able to get themselves ready, Sammy had to attend the service as he was.

Hubby was allocated the task of parking control, ensuring the street was kept clear to allow the hearse and family car to park immediately outside Liz and Paul's house. He took the task altogether too seriously and it resulted in our postman never parking his van in our street again. Once the cars had arrived, we followed the neighbours in a convoy for the crematorium. Arriving about ten minutes early, we joined the other mourners in front of the building to wait for Liz and her family.

I stood alongside Sylvie, a petite, sweet-natured lady in her late seventies. She volunteers at the local hospital, and her hobbies include knitting and doing jigsaws. Conversations with Sylvie usually involve discussing the weather and baking. Without being rude, she is the very definition of a little old lady.

Imagine my shock then, when Sylvie leaned in and told me that she was, 'Fucking sick of Keith pestering her for sex all the time.' That's right, it turns out old Keith wasn't just bothering the furniture; plenty of life left in the old dog yet. Sylvie then offered me some unsolicited wisdom which I have never read in any of Cosmo's Top Ten Sex Tips – and feel free to use this yourself, ladies, when you get to a certain age. A combination of childbirth and aging muscles all have an impact on tightness in certain areas, as I'm sure many of you will be aware. So, Sylvie recommends if your other half is pounding away to no avail, simply cough hard. That's right, a few hearty coughs serve to act as a temporary vaginoplasty, which will finish off your elderly Casanova.

I have never tried so hard not to laugh as I did that day. Part of me thinks that's why Sylvie said it, a bit of mischief to amuse herself. I'm sure I saw a little twinkle in her eye and it made me see her in a completely different light.

As I was being schooled in OAP sex, hubby was also learning more about a neighbour than he cared to. He found himself next to Sammy, and it all started very normally, with standard small talk. After that was out of the way Sammy asked,

'Did you know I used to live in America?'

'No, I didn't know that,' hubby replied.

'Yes, it was wonderful, and then I moved on to Canada. Do you know what we used to do in Canada for fun?'

'No, what did you do Sammy?'

'Well, we used to all put our car keys in a bowl on the table. Then the women would pick a set of keys out, and whoever belonged to that set of keys is who they went home with,' Sammy explained as if it was the most normal thing in the world.

'Can you imagine that now?' he continued. 'At ninety-two, I don't think anyone would be quite as interested. Oh well, I suppose I would just have to go home and see to myself.'

Just as hubby was processing the image of old Sammy rubbing one out, having been rejected at some nursing home swingers party, Sammy decided to share his views on the Japanese. Imagine finding out that your sweet old neighbour was a raging sex fiend, and a closet racist to boot.

A week after the funeral, I was walking out to my car, when through an open window I heard Sylvie have a severe coughing fit. I'm sure I then heard Keith let out a little groan.

CHAPTER EIGHT

Mona

COMING UNSTUCK...

Pregnancy is such a subjective experience. Some women breeze through nine months of glowing, when strangers compliment them on how beautiful their skin is, and how motherhood clearly suits them. Others are not so fortunate. Unrelenting morning sickness, outbreaks of acne, lank, greasy hair, and high blood pressure, are but a few of the symptoms Mother Nature afflicts on some soon-to-be mums.

As a mother of two, I have experienced both sides of the coin. My first pregnancy was amazing, a very mild case of morning sickness in the early weeks, after which I glowed all the way. The first twelve months with our new baby was just as amazing. No sleepless nights, no problems with feeding, and no illness. As young and inexperienced parents, rather than thank our lucky stars about being dealt a good hand, we thought it was down to our Jedi-like parenting skills. Oh, the arrogance. I clearly remember the two of us patting ourselves on the back for achieving a Zen-like level of parenting. Saying things like, 'It's all about setting boundaries and establishing routines.'

Such was our confidence, we planned on having four kids. I mean, our natural gifts shouldn't be limited to just one or two kids, should they? It was on our daughter's first birthday that we decided the time was right to add the second bundle of joy to our little family. As we strolled around the zoo that day, pushing a one-year-old who couldn't even begin to comprehend what a giraffe was, let alone appreciate its majesty, our minds were made up.

We were duped. It turned out that our parenting had played little, or no part, in how easy the first twelve months had been. It was nothing more than luck, pure dumb luck. If my first pregnancy was amazing, my second was hell on earth. I was constantly hungry, but whatever I ate, I either vomited straight back up or it felt as if someone was using a flamethrower directly on my heart. My hair looked like I had been washing it in oil from the chip pan, and my skin broke out in the worst spots.

To make matters worse our daughter clearly sensed the impending pretender to the throne. Like a shark smelling blood in the water, she launched an offensive, and sleepless nights became the norm. I had a tiny human inside of me, draining what little energy reserves I had, whilst his accomplice attacked from the outside. All the self-congratulatory back slapping stopped. There was no more crowing about our natural parenting abilities, and every day we reassured ourselves it was just a blip, life would return to normal after the birth.

I was looking forward to that, because my first birth was wonderful – bobbing about in the birthing pool, some pushing, and then a beautiful 7lb 1oz baby. Hubby was by my side throughout, a rucksack full of my favourite treats, including frozen Capri Sun sachets, at his feet, carefully judging the right time to rub my shoulders and when to back off. They were the best moments of my life.

My second birth, however, was even worse than the pregnancy. Hubby wasn't with me as it was the middle of the night, and we didn't have anyone to look after an angry twenty-two-month-old. The birthing pool was already in use, I didn't have any frozen juice sachets, and I refused all offers of pain relief as I hadn't needed any the first-time round – some of that youthful arrogance remained. With the wisdom of experience, I now know every labour is different, and using pain relief is not a sign of failure, but simple common sense. Unbeknown to me at the time, not only was baby number two almost 2lb heavier, he was also in what is commonly known as the Superman position. That means coming into the world with one of his arms raised above his head, the stance Superman takes when he is in flight. This, obviously, is asking a little more of your vagina than a traditional head first position. By the time the midwives realised what was happening I was screaming at them for an epidural, but alas it was too late. The way I spoke to those women will haunt me until my dying days. My behaviour would have been more at home in a prison riot than a labour ward. To add insult to injury, as the poor midwife held my leg up in the air to relieve the pressure, the baby pressed on my bladder and I pissed all over her. Dignity became a stranger to me that night.

The hospital called hubby at about 1a.m. to inform him of the birth and let him know he could come up for a couple of hours, before we were transferred to the ward. When he arrived, I was having my vagina stitched back together after his son's superhero entrance. That was probably just as well for him, as the first thing he did was to complain about how bad the telly had been that night, moaning he'd had to watch Police Academy 4: Citizens on Patrol. Had I not been in stirrups I think I may have forced him up his own arse in the Superman position.

So, our plans of a perfect family were shattered, and we had to come to terms with the results of creating an arch-nemesis for our daughter. No cute videos exist of our little toddler fawning over her new-born brother. In fact, as I was cradling him on the couch when he was two weeks old, she waddled over, smiled beautifully, turned around and gave him a backwards head-butt that Vinnie Jones would be proud of. Suffice to say, we stopped at two children, and are much humbler regarding our parenting abilities.

All expectant mothers have one thing in common, though, regardless of how smooth the pregnancy or birth. At some point you are going to be in a room, lying on a bed, with strangers staring at your fanny. For most women this isn't as bad as you would imagine, particularly when the pain kicks in. Once those contractions start you'd let the Welsh Male Voice Choir have a peek between your legs, if you thought they could help speed things up. Not that I think a stirring rendition of Myfanwy would have any real effect either way, but you never know.

What may surprise you is the number of women who will not go anywhere near a maternity ward without having had a wax. Even after months of suffering with anything from haemorrhoids to a split pelvis, some women just need to have a hair-free foof. Honestly, there are women who cannot walk without the aid of crutches, literally splitting in two, but they are only worried that someone might see their hairy beaver.

I was no exception, and given my profession, it would have been a bad advert for business to turn up with anything other than a smooth undercarriage. But I had one little problem. I do my own waxing, which ordinarily is fine, but a stomach the size of a blimp made it more difficult than usual. And, a bit like a hairdresser cutting her own hair, I just haven't found a waxer I'm comfortable with. Because I know how the treatment should be done properly, I have little time for bad service in the industry.

Which is why I found myself heavily pregnant, squatting on the floor, thighs burning, as I applied hot wax to my lady garden. If this is something you fancy trying yourself, you will need the following: wax pot with hot wax (obviously), wax sticks and an angled mirror, because unless you are a yoga expert, you will need it to see what you are doing. Lastly, and this is completely optional, a strong light comes in handy. Personally, I use hubby's portable work lamp, which is usually used for illuminating loft spaces. It is very much lighting on an industrial scale, and it does give your vagina the appearance of being part of a West-end stage show. You could put on the greatest hits of the Welsh Male Voice Choir and make your fanny sing along, if you fancied it.

Just one little tip – always ensure you lock the door, or at least make sure that no one else is home. Hubby walked in on me self-waxing once and said, 'Jesus, for a minute there I thought you were recreating the rescue of the Chilean miners.' In my defence this was post-children and being lit up down below like a football stadium at night, is not a good look for anybody. Especially after the Man of Steel has burst his way out of your vag.

So, even heavily pregnant and squatting on the floor, I managed to wax everything around the front with relative ease. Waxing your own ass however, is a lot more difficult even when you aren't pregnant. You can't do it the way you would with a client, it is physically impossible. So, you need to approach from a different angle, and you need to be determined. Once you apply that wax it needs to come off, and any hesitation can lead to a lot of pain. On a client I have this perfected, I can be waxing multiple areas at one time, like a plate spinner keeping several plates in the air. On myself, it's a different technique and I am not nearly as practised. With my thighs burning, and fatigue setting in, I made the disastrous decision to try and apply wax to either side of my butt crack at the same time. The inevitable happened just as I had applied the second strip. My legs gave in, and my ass cheeks closed together, and the wax stuck fast.

Often, when people find themselves with wax stuck on their skin, they try to remove it with heat. However, running a scalding hot bath will only make your situation worse. Fortunately, I knew that the best thing to use for removing wax is oil. You can buy wax removal products that we use in the industry, but if you are in a bind, baby oil works just as well. As I was in the house instead of my treatment room, this was exactly what

I had to hand. So, I carefully climbed into the bath, got onto all fours and gently began massaging baby oil into my ass.

Just as I was pouring out more oil, of course my funny bugger of a husband walked in.

'What's up? You run out of Anusol?' he said.

'Yeah, that's right, I'm out of haemorrhoid cream, so I thought I would rub my arse with baby oil. Now shut up and come and rub this wax off my asshole.'

That is what you call true love. When without question, your hubby massages oil into your partner's ass cheeks until they come unstuck.

Pregnancy changes everything about your relationship with your partner. If you work hard and have a bit of luck it makes it stronger, but make no mistake, nothing is ever the same. We were very young when we decided to have kids, and so was our relationship. On paper everything was against us. For a start I was hubby's first girlfriend, and at twenty-three he was still a virgin. Without going into it too deeply... I wasn't. I'm sure he won't mind me telling you, that the first time he stayed over at my flat it didn't go as planned. I excused myself to go to the bathroom to 'freshen up', and when I returned to the bedroom, wearing my sexiest underwear, he was already in bed with the duvet pulled up to his neck. As I seductively climbed on to the bed and pulled the cover back, I discovered he was still fully clothed, and lying rigid with fear. This was alien to me, usually if a guy got you to the bedroom you didn't have to coax him out of his clothes.

'I've got something to tell you,' he said with a gulp, 'but my friends have told me not to.'

I immediately started running scenarios through my head, each one more outlandish than the last. Maybe I had got my wires crossed and he was just looking for a friend and didn't know how to tell me. Perhaps he was married and wanted to come clean before we went any further. Or he was secretly gay and couldn't get it up for a woman; his body was covered in thick matted hair like a wolf-boy and he had to shave his entire face every day; he had mistaken spray adhesive for his deodorant and was glued into his shirt... Three nipples! That was it, he'd got an extra nipple. Or, oh my God, he didn't have a cock. He lost his cock in a horrific accident, and now out of politeness I was going to have to marry him or look like a cruel bitch.

Then he said it. 'I'm a virgin.'

It turned out he was born with a tight foreskin and should have been circumcised as a child, but his mum was given bad advice by the doctor, so he wasn't. Sex was impossible, so he elected to be circumcised when he was twenty-one. By this time, his virginity had gone from a source of embarrassment to something he valued, and didn't just want to give away. Something he chose to tell me, as I was straddling him in my sexiest underwear. Apparently, he was pretty sure I was The One, but he wanted to be, 'absolutely positive', before we went all the way.

Suddenly, I felt very naked: less heated tryst and more talent show audition. I had never met a man who didn't take sex when it was offered up on a plate, and honestly, I think this was what made me realise he was different. Although he did nearly undo his White Knight image when he said,

'We can still do other stuff, if you like?'

'What like?

He shrugged his shoulders. 'Blowjob?'

There was no blowjob that night, just a long cuddle. But everything went at a hundred miles an hour after that. We both decided we were each other's One, and at three months in, that youthful arrogance made us think it was the right time to have kids. Twelve weeks! I've taken longer to decide on wallpaper.

A conservative estimate of six to twelve months to get pregnant seemed fair. That would give us enough time to get to know each other better, look for a bigger place – as a one bed flat wasn't ideal, and maybe even go away on holiday together.

Four days.

It took him two years to build a workroom that is little more than an outbuilding, but he created life in four days. Virgin bollocks ended up being the most virile man I have ever met. It wasn't just a fluke either, as he did it again with our second. His theory is a little depressing, but his logic seems sound. You see, he did everything wrong for a man who wants a high sperm count. He was overweight, his diet was atrocious, he drank, and he never exercised. I know, a real catch – why did you want to have kids with him, I hear you ask? As well as being a decent guy, he is honestly the funniest person I have ever met. I never wanted to settle down, but I couldn't stop myself from loving him.

So, how did he do it? Well, he was a real tosspot. His tight foreskin meant he had always been too scared to let any girl touch his turtle-neck wearing sausage. He had to develop a very specific way of pleasuring himself with as little movement as possible. And it turned out he was quite fond of it – had he fitted a dynamo to his wrist he could have made a fortune selling power to the national grid.

If having kids is part of your life plan then take it from me, marry a wanker; apparently the more often a man ejaculates, the healthier the sperm. His must have had the stamina of Sir Mo Farah.

Women who are pregnant with their first child can be a little precious, quite often wrapped up in the belief they are the first woman to experience this wondrous thing. Ironically, the very thing that they deem so precious, will very quickly send them back down to earth with a bump. When you see a woman on her second pregnancy onwards, she is usually just relieved to have got herself dressed in the morning, and if fortune favours her, the chance to go to the toilet alone.

My client Annabel has two children and is currently pregnant with her third. Annabel is Dutch and moved here when her husband got a work. I don't know why, but she insists on bringing all her children to her waxing appointments. I get why she brings the third one – they pretty much come as a package just now – but the first two are surplus to requirements. This may seem a little harsh, but I never took my kids anywhere if it wasn't appropriate. I am also baffled as to why Annabel persists with her waxing, as in every other area of her appearance she has given up. And I am truly not being judgemental, I have been there. I remember sitting in public toilets whilst my daughter unlocked and opened the cubicle door to reveal me like some sad gameshow prize. Leggings and knickers round my knees, hair not having been brushed for weeks, food and vomit stains dotted all over my clothes, odd socks, and not a lick of makeup. Being a mum is the most thankless, exhausting job you can do. So, I get it.

But watching Annabel getting a wax, is almost as exhausting as waxing her. Her eldest child is four and the youngest eighteen months. The last time she was in, she allowed the four-year old to wander freely, whilst the eighteen-month-old stood next to the treatment bed, screaming at her. Without a word, Annabel scooped him off the floor, exposed her left breast, which the red-faced tot hungrily attached itself to, and began singing a Dutch nursery song. Times like this make me appreciate just how surreal my job is. As that broken woman lay naked on my bed, bleeding from her nipple, singing in a language I didn't understand, I saw that look of horror in her eyes. The acceptance that life will never be the same again, and worst of all you have done it to yourself.

I would like to make it very clear, though, that I do love my children very much and if I had the chance to do it all over again I would. But maybe I would book a holiday first.

Four bloody days.

Chapter Nine

Mrs Armour

Can you wait behind...

In the early days, before Superspunk finished the build (during which he could have impregnated me 182.5 times), working from home was a little awkward. My dining room, serving as a temporary treatment room, was at the very end of our hallway, so clients had to walk right through the house. This meant that for most of the time I was working, hubby had to keep the kids in the confines of the living room.

Our house is a modern build and has paper thin walls, through which noise permeates from one room to the other. Between the stereo in my workroom and hubby keeping the TV on in the living room, the kids never overheard anything untoward from my more colourful clients. Hubby was also very good at keeping my clients from tripping over little people as they came and went and toilet breaks were carried out with military precision, so that nobody crossed paths in our narrow hall. I know some people thought we took it too far, after all, clients knew they were coming to my home, but we felt that a personal treatment deserved to be as private as possible. The kids were too young to understand what mummy did, they just knew that when I was working, they had to be on their very best behaviour.

Despite the restrictions, our set up worked very well, and life was good. That was until the kids and I bumped into one of my clients, Clara, in the supermarket. I had told her all about them, mostly high praise, but on bad days there were some harsher reviews. In my experience, parents who do nothing but gush about their kids are not to be trusted. Invariably they are unrealistic, and their kids are the troublemakers due to lack of discipline.

Anyway, Clara loved kids and was excited to finally be meeting mine. You can always tell when someone is used to talking to young children, in that they speak in a more sing-song tone, words are exaggerated, and facial expressions are animated. Equally, you can tell when someone isn't used to it. They tend to clam up slightly, not knowing exactly what to say. It is not dissimilar to watching Prince Philip meeting foreign dignitaries: you know they are going to say something inappropriate, it's just a question of when.

As much as Clara loved kids, she didn't have any. Nor did she have any nieces or nephews, so she was very much in the second camp. So of course, she said something completely ridiculous to my four-year-old daughter.

'Well, hello, it's nice to meet you. I'm Clara. I've heard all about you and you have probably heard me screaming from your mum's torture chamber in the house.'

This was met with a blank expression, as most of the sentence didn't make any sense to a four-year-old who was usually spoken to as you would an elderly relative whose mind had wandered a little. It was delivered as though to an acquaintance Clara had bumped into in the pub, no sing-song tone, and no animated gestures to hold her attention. It made *me* chuckle a little, though I thought nothing more of it after we had said our goodbyes.

The following day, I received a call from Mrs Armour, my daughter's nursery teacher. She was phoning to express some concerns about something said in class, and to ask if I could wait behind after pick-up to discuss it.

My first thought was that one of the kids had learned a new swear word and then taught the rest of the class. It had happened the year before, when our beautiful three-year-old picked up the word 'fuck'. Unless you have a stick up your ass, this situation raises a dilemma. Part of you thinks it horrific, that your sweet child has heard a bad word and lost some of her innocence. But another part thinks, 'This is hilarious, should I film it and put it on Facebook?' Watching a tiny human exclaim, 'Oh fuck,' as they knock down their tower of building blocks, or muttering, 'Fuck this,' when you tell them it's time for bed, does evoke an involuntary snigger. Plus, there is something oddly impressive about three-year-olds using expletives in the proper context, especially when many of them are still filling their pull-up nappies. Panic does set in very quickly, however, as you most certainly don't want anybody to think that this is how you speak at home.

Like everything in parenting, there is conflicting advice on how to deal with this situation. The first option is to ignore it and hope it goes away. Personally, I think this reaction is flawed, as if left unchecked the child thinks it is acceptable and sees no reason to stop. Secondly, you can try and talk to the child and explain why this is unacceptable, and hope they understand. The problem with that is in asking a three-year-old to comprehend something far beyond them. Thirdly, you can chastise them and hopefully frighten them into not using the word. Unfortunately, most three-year-olds relish doing things they are not meant to, and all you are doing is adding an element of excitement to the situation.

This sums up parenting perfectly: you weigh up all the options, find there is no correct answer and all you are left with is, 'Fuck this.'

So, there I was, sitting on a tiny chair – they only have tiny chairs in nursery class – in front of the teacher's desk. The whole scene was ridiculous. I looked even bigger than normal, with beads of sweat forming on my forehead because I could feel the teensy, plastic chair starting to buckle under frame and was trying to take some of my weight on my legs.

The C-word would have been preferable to what happened next.

'Mrs Pearson, I have asked you to come in to discuss something that your daughter said in class today,' Mrs Armour said with a very serious look on her face.

'Is it the F-word again?' I asked. 'I really thought that was under control now.'

'No, I'm afraid not.' she continued. 'It was something far more concerning.'

My mind raced. Anything but the C-word, I thought. I can deal with 'shit' or 'bastard', but if it's the C-word then I won't be able to take my daughter out of the house for months. Sweat ran down my forehead onto my nose. I started thinking of her classmates, playing an imaginary game of Guess Who in my head, trying to work out the most likely culprit that could have taught my little angel this horrific word. Ryan had taught her 'fuck', but he moved schools at the end of last year, so he was off the hook. What about little Jonny? He was always at the football with his dad, he could easily have picked it up at the stadium. Then there was Matt, he had a much older brother whose friends hung around at the house, smoking in the garage. Older teenagers always swore to make themselves look cool, didn't they? I tried to remember being a teenager, but it's a lifetime ago.

Oh bugger, what about hubby? Did he use the C-word? I delved deep into my memory bank to try and recall if I had ever heard him drop the C-bomb. This could be embarrassing. Wait, was it me? Did I say it? Shit, it must be me. I'm such a bad mum, I wondered if Mrs Armour would phone social services?

This is what having kids does to you. The day they are born you begin a spiralling descent into self-doubt induced madness.

I noticed Mrs Armour's eyes wander to my forehead and realised the sweating was making me look guilty.

I looked over to the far corner of the room where my beautiful daughter was playing with the Lego. I was almost manic; this was how I'd remember her, I thought, playing happily, unaware how her mother failed her before she was taken away to another family, one that didn't use the C-word.

'How are things at home, Mrs Pearson?' She tilted her head to one side, a quizzical look on her face.

'Fine?' It was almost a question rather than an answer. 'Great, I mean, everything's great,' I corrected myself.

'And how are things with Mr Pearson?'

I couldn't believe it – it was hubby, he who is so bloody pious about bad language. Well, I would have some choice words for him when I got home.

'He's great too. Everybody is great. How are you?'

'A little concerned, Mrs Pearson, if I am being honest. Your daughter is a very happy child and is a credit to you and your husband. However, she told the class today at story time, that her mummy has a torture chamber in her house, where she hurts people and makes them scream. Can you explain why she would say this?'

Bloody Clara and her big mouth. At four-years-old she might not have understood the sentence, but she certainly was able to parrot it. Fortunately, once I explained my job, and what Clara had said about it, the relief on Mrs Armour's face was almost palpable. Apparently, she had been looking down the barrel of some serious paperwork, and some awkward conversations with senior management.

Mrs Armour has ended up being a regular visitor to my torture chamber, and to this day asks me to book her in for her next session 'on the rack'. Hubby says it's astounding how I never miss an opportunity to drum up new business.

The rest of both kids' time in nursery was uneventful – save for an impressive display of gluttony from our son. Hubby picked him up one day after class and was driving him into town, when without warning he projectile vomited all over the back of the car. (Apparently, the smell was particularly bad, fortunately for me hubby had cleaned it all up.) Hubby popped back to nursery to check if there was a sickness bug doing the rounds. There wasn't; just the record of a greedy pig.

Located at the back wall of the classroom, was a snack table from which the kids, allowed one snack each, were trusted to take only their fair share. That day the snack had been cheese, our son's favourite. So, he pulled up a chair, ate the entire class's supply of cheddar, then pebble-dashed it all over the car.

That's parenting in a nutshell. It doesn't matter whether it's what's coming out of their mouths or what they are putting, you are left to clean up the mess.

Chapter Ten

Samantha

Losing her marbles...

I was so relieved when I came out of my meeting with Mrs Armour that I was ambushed with the stealth of a lioness. With her prey in sight, Mrs Jewson, the headteacher, launched her offensive. Usually, I would have outmanoeuvred her and bolted like a mighty wildebeest, but that day I was more like a lame zebra, easy pickings.

'Mrs Pearson, so lovely to see you,' Mrs Jewson said, with her trademark disingenuous smile. 'You have actually saved me from having to call you.'

I readied myself for what the school mums dubbed the Bullshit Blitz. Mrs Jewson was one of the falsest people you could ever have the displeasure of meeting. More faces than the town clock, as my old Grampa would say. The problem was that stupid people fell for it; she finessed parents of limited intelligence into doing what she wanted. Until then I hadn't been on her radar, having only met her a handful of times when I volunteered as a parent helper. Clearly something had changed.

'Can I just say, Mrs Pearson, what an absolute delight your daughter is to have as part of our family here at the school,' she schmoozed.

Psychology 101, build up a rapport with your victim, make them think you have a connection.

'And I can't thank you enough for all your precious time, given up helping in the nursery. A lot of our activities would be impossible without the assistance of our wonderful parents, like yourself.'

Stroke their ego and watch them puff out their chest with self-importance. Let them think they are an integral part in how the school runs.

'I couldn't help but notice what a natural leader you are, and how the other parents and staff respond to your larger than life character.'

Soften them up for the kill, lather them in compliments until their guard has dropped completely. Ordinarily, I would have seen what she was doing. I would have cut her off, made my excuses, and legged it. But I was just grateful that my child didn't know the C-word and Social Services weren't arranging to inspect my treatment-room-cum-torture-chamber.

'A position has opened for Chair of the PTA due to Mrs Williamson's sudden issue with her nerves.'

An issue that was largely caused by Mrs Jewson and her increasing demands upon Mrs Williamson, I thought. Dawn Williamson was a lovely woman, but she could not say no. The headteacher used her like Punch, a puppet to do all the dirty work that she didn't want to.

'I was just wondering if you have ever considered running for a position on the board of the PTA?'

Truth be told, it was more than the PTA. Our school was operating the PTA and the Parent Council as a joint body, which was a serious case of flouting protocol. The PTA have the responsibility of raising funds for a school, and the Parent Council is tasked with issues regarding its running. The Parent Council wields far more power and should be included in all the big decisions regarding the school, from staff selection to the spending of grants. Mrs Jewson preferred them to operate as one body as it meant Dawn Williamson oversaw both, her strings pulled to do the headteacher's bidding.

I never even considered that this was how MRs Jewson was looking at me: a weak-minded individual, who would nod along and sign off on whatever was put in front of me. But before I knew what was happening, I had somehow agreed to attend the PTA meeting that night.

It was weird being in an empty school. Claire, the Vice Chair, was running the meeting, her face frozen with a rabbit in the headlights expression. Claire was an inoffensive soul but had even less about her than Dawn. I honestly expected Mrs Jewson to put her arm up the back of Claire's jumper and work her like a ventriloquist's dummy.

Claire and the Board sat at the front, facing a collective of about thirty parents of kids from various year groups. As I am such a gab, I already knew over half of the room, which was not the norm for a parent from the nursery, as a matter of fact nursery parents rarely attended the meetings at all. A further quick headcount told me that of the fortyish people in the room, I regularly waxed six of their vaginas and two willies. Three of them were on the Board.

Ordinarily in a group situation (which, to be fair, is rare), people don't usually let on how they know me, beyond a knowing smile and a nod of the head. This was the case tonight, except for Daniella, one of the Primary Three mums. She always made a show of pointing to herself, then me, and then her vagina, followed up with a massively exaggerated wink – her subtle way of letting me know she needed a wax. To those in the room who didn't know what I did for a living it must have appeared that she was very openly, and very aggressively, coming on to me at a PTA meeting. Not that it would bother Daniella, who loves a bit of controversy.

When Mrs Jewson asked if there were any volunteers to fill the role of Chair, she fixed me with the oddest stare I have ever seen from a human. Her face strained to keep her Joker-like smile in place; it was like watching an android trying to replicate emotion. Her head started to gently shake from side to side with the effort of it all. I half expected her to say, 'Look into my eyes, not around my eyes, look into my eyes,' as she attempted to hypnotise me into signing my life away.

It was immediately clear that the PTA was in disarray and lacked any leadership whatsoever, so I still don't know why I put my hand up that night. Sense of duty, perhaps, because I knew my kids would be there for almost the next decade. Or, pity for the broken souls that sat before me on the board, maybe. Hubby said it was because I knew Mrs Jewson was underestimating me, and I never like being played.

Whatever the reason, I volunteered and was duly nominated and seconded, and before you knew it, I was the new Chair of the PTA.

The role came with all the problems you would expect: a dictatorial headteacher, who was only happy when she got her own way; unrealistic parents, who massively overestimated their own children's ability, expecting bizarre forms of recognition for their less than impressive achievements. One mother petitioned the school to have a parade to celebrate her dreadful child's success in swimming. Even if her child was likeable, it would have been an outlandish suggestion.

On top of the normal problems encountered by a member of the Board, I had additional issues. As I explained earlier, people treat my workroom like a confessional, which means that most of my clients who were members of the PTA had told me their darkest secrets. They had done so never imagining that our kids would end up at the same school. To be fair, most of the confessions were relatively pedestrian: one woman enjoyed anal sex with her husband, another overlooked her neighbour's bedroom and had developed a habit of watching them have sex. All very tame, and no way that I would blab.

Samantha, however, was a different story. Sam started coming to me long before we met at the school. Dripping in jewellery and designer gear, she drove a Range Rover and rarely talked about anything other than herself. I had been waxing her for five months before she even mentioned she had kids. Very much the definition of a kept woman, her husband worked on the oil rigs, whilst she stayed at home and got her nails and hair done.

From her first appointment she bragged about how much money her man earned, and I assumed her appointments were booked to coincide with his return, as his reward for bringing home the bacon. It was only when she mentioned she was pissed off her husband's flight had been delayed, that the truth came out.

'Oh, that's a shame,' I said. 'Does that mean he won't be getting home till later?'

'What do you mean? I'm talking about his flight *out*. I had to put up with him for an extra three hours this morning,' she spat angrily.

'Oh sorry, I assumed you came and got waxed for him coming home.'

'Ha, no chance, I don't even wash it when he's coming home, don't want him getting any ideas.' She chuckled.

She bragged that as her husband was out drilling the seabed in the North Sea, she was at home getting drilled by her personal trainer in the marital bed – with a perfectly smooth, hair-free fanny, courtesy of me.

Most people in her situation would be very wary of pissing me off, for the slimmest chance I might get angry and inadvertently let slip her extra marital activities. Not Sam, though, the very definition of a diva. At every meeting of the PTA she turned up to cause drama; she did it everywhere she went. I'm sure you know the type: any attention is good attention, so long as all eyes are on her.

The only place she didn't behave like a complete twat was during her waxing appointments. Yes, she was still a total show off, but at points you got to see the girl who grew up on the council estate. Just a fleeting appearance, before the need to crow took over.

As with most mean girls, Sam liked to travel in a pack and she always rocked up to the PTA with her two henchwomen, Sarah and Janine. Like Draco Malfoy with Vincent Crabbe and Gregory Goyle (I am a Harry Potter nut, full of analogies from the wizarding world), she was very much the brains of the outfit. I don't know exactly what the other two brought to the party, I can only imagine it was their ability to agree blindly with Sam. They too were women of leisure, and with nothing but money and time on their hands, both Sarah and Janine had their fair share of skeletons in their closets.

Sarah's husband ran a construction firm, and he was rarely home. Janine's husband was a bit sketchy and nobody really knew what he did for a living, except that it paid exceptionally well. In our town, if you make a lot of money from a less than obvious source – we're an aging population so this refers to banking, retail, medicine or law – you are immediately labelled a drug dealer.

Anyway, back to the PTA. Mrs Jewson regretted asking me to join almost immediately. My first course of action was to separate the PTA and Parent Council. As serving Chairperson of the PTA, I then stood for Chairperson of the newly formed Parent Council. I was duly elected and set about convincing the best suited parents to fill the roles of Vice Chair, Treasurer and Secretary. I was thrilled to have one of the Primary 2 mum's as Vice Chair. Gina was a high flyer in finance, working for one of the largest global accounting firms. She was highly intelligent, focused, and most of all, fierce. Doug – owner of one of the willies in the PTA that I waxed – took up the position of Treasurer. Smart as a whip and with a wicked sense of humour, he made the meetings more bearable. Emma stepped up as Secretary, she ran her own small business and was super organised.

I immediately arranged for the meetings of the two separate groups to take place on different nights, and then drew up a constitution for the Parent Council. This meant that each group could concentrate solely on what their own purpose was.

Sam was furious with this new development, as it meant she had to give up two evenings of doing nothing, to come and be a thorn in my side. And it was at one of the Parent Council meetings that the terrible trio came unstuck.

The school had been awarded a grant for outdoor learning. The remit was rather broad and there was scope for the parents to have an input as to how the money was spent. The consensus was on a Trim Trail, an outdoor timber obstacle course, designed to improve fitness and flexibility. It is suitable for all age groups and there was a perfect spot in the playground for it.

Sam had other ideas, like a bespoke marble sundial, which Sarah's husband's company would supply and fit. It was a ridiculous suggestion, stemming from her recently developed obsession with Venice, following on from a three amigos' weekend away. We had all been bored senseless with tales of the opulent hotels in the Grand Canal; ancient buildings with marble floors, marble columns, marble tables, marble vanity units. To listen to them you would think the Venetians were cutting about wearing bloody marble shoes.

I quickly dismissed the suggestion, pointing out that there was absolutely no benefit to the children of a marble sundial.

Sam was furious at my lack of respect. 'Surely the benefit would be in adding a little culture into their lives. But I wouldn't expect someone like you to understand anything about that,' she seethed.

'Yeah, Mona, you're just a waxer, we wouldn't expect you to know anything about the finer things in life. We just think adding a touch of class to the school will give the kids some self-respect,' Janine added.

Before I even had the chance to formulate a response in my mind, Daniella jumped up from her chair.

'Who the fuck are you talking to, you wee skank?' she raged, but at Sam rather than Janine. 'The only culture you know about is the one the doctor took from your nasty minge to test for chlamydia. You know, the chlamydia you caught from pumping your personal trainer whilst your husband was away.' She pointed angrily at Sam.

It would appear Sam's secret was not as well kept as she thought.

'And you, with your finer things.' Jabbing her finger in Janine's direction. 'Do you mean all the fancy crap you buy with your man's money? The money he makes from punting gear? Where's your self-respect?' Daniella sat back down. 'You're not getting a bloody sundial,' she said quietly.

Sam and her cronies never came to any meetings after that, and Daniella's next wax was on the house.

Chapter Eleven

Pauline

Let's Get Physical...

As far as clients go, Pauline is completely normal. A happily married mother of two, who works in a bank. Other than the normal problems that come with having kids, her life is totally drama free. Her husband John is a lawyer and he likes to play golf at the weekend.

I don't have any embarrassing stories about Pauline, she's just partly responsible for one of the most embarrassing things that has ever happened to me.

Well, technically, not *responsible*, merely the catalyst, and if I'm being honest it wasn't something that happened to me, rather something I did.

Pauline's dad died from cancer shortly after her first child was born. She struggled badly with grief that almost consumed her. John suggested it might be useful if she could find something to channel this emotion into. Wanting to do something positive, she decided she was going to hold a fundraiser in memory of her dad, to support a local cancer charity.

It was important to her that the event was something fun that people wanted to attend, rather than feeling obliged. As a talented singer and keen karaoke performer, she decided on a Stars In Their Eyes competition. For those of you too young to remember, Stars In Their Eyes was an ITV programme in the nineties and early noughties, hosted by Matthew Kelly, an affable, bearded gentleman, rarely seen on screen now. Contestants, who were members of the public, not professional singers, were given a makeover then imitated their chosen singing act. Some were better than others; to this day the Freddie Mercury still tours as a professional Freddie Mercury imitator.

Pauline threw herself into organising the event. She secured a venue with a stage and cheap bar. Her brother-in-law, a mobile DJ, provided the sound system and lights, and her cousin agreed to fill the role of Matthew Kelly. Her aunts were organising the buffet – a lovely selection of hot and cold foods – and John helped her decorate the room.

Between family and friends, she quickly sold all the tickets, enough to cover the cost of the venue and a healthy donation to the charity. To boost funds further a raffle was held on the night, with prizes donated from local businesses.

The inaugural Stars In Their Eyes charity night was a massive success, and everybody thoroughly enjoyed themselves. So much so, that Pauline, rightly proud, decided she was going to make it an annual event.

I first met Pauline just after she had held the third S.I.T.E night and raised a substantial sum. She had come for a wax after her friend from work had recommended me and it didn't take long for us to talk about the charity night and how Pauline was struggling to find new performers. Although it was a bit of fun, she was keen to provide decent singers. After all, people were buying tickets and they weren't expecting drunken wailing for their money. Two of the same singers had appeared at all three nights, and she was keen for fresh blood.

It just so happened that the week before I had won a karaoke competition in one of our local pubs. I must admit, I am very much a frustrated performer. I love singing and am certainly no wallflower. My go-to song is Tina Turner's, Proud Mary and I've got the Tina strut perfected. Pauline had already heard from her friend about my vocal triumph and was hoping to recruit me for S.I.T.E four.

Bizarrely, she asked me to audition for it, there and then, whilst waxing her fanny. I gave her my best rendition of Get Happy by Judy Garland and she signed me up on the spot. Words cannot explain how happy I was – in my excitement I *may* have exaggerated and told people I had been signed to a label. Although technically I wasn't getting paid, I now classed myself as a professional singer.

With the best part of a year before my debut performance as a pro, I had plenty of time to perfect my act. Of course, I was going to be Tina, there was no doubt in my mind. Everywhere I went I channelled The Queen of Rock 'n' Roll.

Squats were the order of the day; the strut was going to need some serious thigh power to do it proper justice. The only doubt I had was the hair: did I wear a wig or fully commit and go for the Tina cut? It would be a bold move to make for just one night, but if something is worth doing, it's worth doing right.

After months of research, practise, and several temper tantrums (all good divas must occasionally have tantrums, or they won't be taken seriously), I received devastating news. Pauline's sister-in-law, Stacey, the DJ's wife, was insisting *she* perform as Tina. While Stacey had performed at every event, she wasn't the strongest of singers, but a concession was made as her husband supplied all the audio equipment. Pauline felt she just couldn't say no, so instead, she asked me to swap and sing as Adele, who Stacey was meant to be originally.

I'm not going to lie, I was gutted. I was grateful for the timing, though, as had she called me two days later, I would have been sporting Tina's famous 80's mullet, having decided that the wig would have been a cop out.

Instead of Proud Mary, I was going to be Rolling in the Deep, Adele's classic from 2011. Although upsetting, this was a mere speed bump for a professional, which in my head, I was still pretending to be.

It was only when Pauline phoned me to book in a slot for my sound check the day before the competition, that I realised this was not a standard karaoke. After the sound check, we had to film a short clip about ourselves and give a few clues as to who we might be performing as – exactly as happened on the show. The clip would be played out as we were being introduced by fake Matthew Kelly. Other people had prepared props, backing dancers, and were coming fully dressed as their chosen act, whereas I was just going to wear a black dress and put on a bit of slap.

I had to up my game.

Accordingly, a friend who is a stylist sorted my hair, and my make up was done courtesy of one of my clients, who worked wonders. To be fair, the black dress I already had was perfect, so no change was made there.

On the day of the show, the nerves hit. This was totally alien to me, as I had always loved performing. I repeatedly told hubby that I was going to pull out, and tried to convince him to phone Pauline and tell her I was sick. He reminded me that I had bought a table, and invited my friends, and grandparents. By cancelling, I would be disappointing them all, the sanctimonious sod pointed out. I *was* keen, though, for my grampa to see me perform, since he rarely got the chance. He was also a seasoned karaoke singer, a Sinatra man, and if I had thought ahead, I would have tried to convince him to sign up.

After a restless night, and a nervous day, I called on one of my old friends for assistance. She has never let me down, through the sad times and happy, the ups and the downs. It didn't matter what was happening in my life I knew I could rely on her. Originally from Italy, her name is Pinot Grigio, and the more time I spend with her, the better things seem. She made quite an early appearance that day and I'm not going to lie, she was being quite mischievous.

By the time Gran and Grampa arrived, my nerves had dissipated and been replaced with altogether too much confidence. You know that drunk way you get before you even go out? When your friends are looking at you and thinking, *Mona's not going to make it to the club tonight.* I was that level of drunk at 4pm.

Most people would stop at that point and try to do some damage limitation. A couple of strong coffees, a bite to eat, perhaps. But Pinot was in my ear, 'Why don't we invite Sambuca over?' Our other Italian friend. 'We haven't seen her in ages.'

By the time we arrived at the venue I was superstar drunk. I all but kicked the doors off their hinges, bursting in like Liam Gallagher.

As I was one of the performers, we arrived half an hour before the audience was due to start coming in. I could see Pauline was a little concerned about my condition, but she had a bigger problem on her hands. Her cousin, a.k.a. fake Matthew Kelly, had come down with food poisoning and was unable to fulfil his duties. At very short notice she had arranged for one of her neighbours to step in, and he was definitely more Jim Davidson than Matthew Kelly.

With me being so drunk, Jim became my new best friend. Almost immediately, I confided in him that I spend all day waxing fannies and balls. On the other hand, hubby took an immediate dislike to him, probably because he was sober and could see Jim for the tosser he was. Hubby doesn't drink. Not anymore anyway. He wasn't a bad drunk, but he was unpredictable, his filter between brain and mouth disappearing completely when he was inebriated. He literally could say anything to anyone, a lack of control that bothered him, so he stopped drinking altogether. It tends to make him a classic boring bastard on a night out, though what he lacks in fun, he more than makes up for by being able to drive us home at the end of the night.

My guests took their places at the table I had bought and began playing catch up with the wine. All but hubby and my grampa, that is. Grampa isn't averse to a drink the way hubby is, it's just that he was also a designated driver that night. My grampa grew up in one of the poorest areas of one of the poorest cities, during one of the toughest times this country has ever lived through. He lived beside some of the roughest characters imaginable, yet without doubt, he is the most prudish person I have ever known. Not in a stuck up, looking down on people, kind of way, he just doesn't have any time for bad language, toilet humour, or innuendo. Grampa is a proper gentleman. As such, the next six hours of his life were going to be exceptionally difficult. Everything that my grampa detested, fake Jim Davidson loved. Jim was a loudmouth and if he wasn't swearing, he was indulging in the most skin-crawling innuendo, or straight-out smut. I, of course, was totally oblivious, backstage and indulging in the wine supplied for the performers.

The venue had a bar on the back wall, with the tables and chairs laid out in front of it, beyond that was a reasonable sized dance floor, and then the stage. The dance floor was to be kept clear as a couple of the acts would be utilising it. The backstage room was adjacent to the bar, so the acts had to make their way through the audience to the stage.

Once the room was full and everyone had taken their seats, the first act made his way to the front. He was last year's winner and wouldn't be competing again, he was simply open proceedings. As such, he didn't have to speak to Jim, for which I'm sure he was very grateful.

I was up fourth and by that time Jim had made quite an impression. Homophobic, sexist, and sexual comments were very much his style. Worryingly, he seemed to be going down quite well with a few of the older members of the audience. As I rocked up to the stage, well and truly buoyed by the booze, I realised I told Jim far too much about myself.

'This next girl spends all day with cocks in her hand and touching women's fannies. I've told her I'll be her apprentice, but only for the birds. She's in tonight with Gran and Grampa – where are you, Grampa? Put your hand up. There he is! Hi, Grampa, you having fun? Look at him there, the old boy hasn't had his balls waxed since the war. Isn't that right, Grampa?'

Hubby said later that his arse had never been clenched so tightly as it was whilst sat next to Grampa, praying that Jim would shut up. Grampa apparently feigned deafness, far too decent a man to cause a scene, and for whatever reason, Jim actually approached Grampa during the break to apologise for what he had said. Hubby cut him off, though, and politely suggested that he get going, whilst the going was good.

Alcohol consumption aside, I did very well and got through to the final. It was me and Olivia Newton John, who was singing Physical.

Olivia had gone all out, full 1980's leotard and headband, and she had also brought backing dancers, two vertically challenged muscle men from her gym. They were wearing nothing but short shorts and fake tan. As she sang and gyrated, they struck poses behind her, flexing their muscles as if this was the moment they had been waiting for since they lifted that first dumbbell.

It went down to the wire, and the general feedback suggested that I was the better singer, but she swung it on showmanship and was declared the winner. As the victor she got to perform again and close the show.

Olivia and her tiny Schwarzeneggers took up position backstage, waiting for the intro to cue the start of their performance. As the music started they bounded out to the dancefloor – at exactly the same time as my booze-addled brain decided that I wasn't quite finished either. Yes, a decision had been made and it was not in my favour, but I wasn't going to let that stop me. I thought, if you can't beat 'em, join 'em.

As I stalked behind the diminutive strongmen in the high heels that made me close to 6' 4" tall, I dwarfed them by about a foot. And as Olivia turned to face the audience, she was greeted with the sight of me bringing up the rear, like a newborn giraffe. When I passed the table where hubby and my grandparents were seated, I grinned at them with the kind of manic smile only seen on someone who has lost all their senses but still thinks they are making good choices.

As Olivia did her best to keep her composure, I attempted to slide into choreography I had not learned – and it showed. I descended into little more than molesting two barely-dressed, muscle-bound, dwarves. I looked like a dishevelled King Kong Adele.

I was slut dropping, a dance move made famous by, well, sluts, which is kind of like a squat, but you go much deeper, and you open your legs. Bearing in mind I was wearing a fitted dress, I was flashing my Spanx to everybody, including my grampa. By this point, I'm sure he was wishing he'd stayed at home and watched Columbo.

Hubby, who is usually very laid back, was clearly furious. Well, to everyone else he was clearly furious, to me, he was enjoying the best performance of my life, and the crowd were loving it, too.

I still wish I could convince myself that was how the night ended: two acts coming together to provide an epic close for the show, me universally loved for being a good sport and assisting the winner in her moment in the limelight. Unfortunately, pictures soon surfaced of me straddling what turned out to be a sixty-five-year-old grandfather, all be it in amazing shape, flashing my massive knickers, with the angriest-looking Olivia Newton John you have ever seen, in the background.

I wasn't invited to perform at the next charity event and I doubt I ever will be again. Occasionally, as I'm drifting off to sleep, I have another flashback to that fateful night and a cold shiver runs down my spine.

I would love to say that Pinot Grigio and I stopped being friends after that, but, well, don't we all have that one friend we just can't say no to?

Chapter Twelve

Michael

Flying carpet ride...

At Michael's first appointment he was exceptionally nervous. This was odd, I thought, given he was an airline pilot, and I had always assumed pilots had nerves of steel. Being responsible for hundreds of people's lives, whilst captaining a flying fuel tank at 30,000 feet, must be up there in terms of bum-clenching careers.

At each first appointment I go through a consultation, part of which is explaining the treatment to the client. Once this is complete, I ask the client to undress and make themselves comfortable on the bed, before excusing myself to the waiting room to allow them some privacy. After a minute or two, I shout through the door to make sure the client is ready, and when I re-enter, I expect to find them positioned on the bed, with the supplied towel draped over their mid-section.

Michael's nerves had clearly got the better of him, and he hadn't paid attention to what I had asked him to do. So, when he shouted through that he was ready, and I went back into the room, instead of finding him flat on his back, modesty covered, I was confronted with him standing at the side of the bed, completely naked.

This threw me for three reasons. Firstly, he had removed his t-shirt, which was unnecessary as he was only getting his cock and balls waxed. Secondly, and more disconcertingly, he had kept his socks on (so, not completely naked, I suppose), which weirded me out – no one should *ever* be seen with just socks on. Getting dressed, should be adorned in a minimum of underpants before socks go on, and when undressing, socks get removed before pants. Imagine having an accident with just your socks on – having to be rescued, completely naked but with toasty warm toes. It would be excruciating. Anyway, thirdly, I nearly didn't realise he *was* completely naked, as Michael is the single most hairy person I have ever seen. Honestly, he was so hairy he could have been an extra in Gorillas in the Mist. I was half expecting Dian Fossey to appear and start documenting his wax.

I don't know if you remember a TV show from the nineties, called Ally McBeal? Actress Calista Flockhart played the title character, a young attorney who has regular fantasy sequences in her mind, whilst having conversations with clients or colleagues. This often led to hilarious consequences, as elements of her fantasy are inadvertently brought into the conversation.

This is something I very much suffer from. I will often glaze over, fleetingly leaving reality before returning with a thump, sometimes having said something out loud without realising it.

I will digress to give you an example. I was standing in a queue in the supermarket, patiently waiting my turn. There was an elderly lady in front of me and she was taking an age sorting her coupons. On the belt, I had a crate of Irn-Bru, (Scotland's greatest export, not whisky, which most people believe), the tagline for the drink, 'It's Phenomenal', written in large letters across the top of the crate. This was the last thing I saw before glazing over. My eyes fixed on the fizzy juice, but my mind was a million miles away, giving me a thousand-yard stare. In real time these blanks don't last long, but to me they feel much longer. On this occasion, as my mind was getting ready for a landing back to earth, the lines between fantasy and reality were blurred, so at the top of my voice I shouted, 'It's Phenomenal!'

It took a moment to register I'd actually shouted this aloud. It was the old lady's face – as if I'd pissed on the floor – that first alerted me and then, as I slowly looked around, every single checkout came to a stop, staff and customers alike taking time out of their day to look at the lunatic who was shouting at the top of her lungs. The only thing I could think to do was point at the cans, shrug my shoulders, and say, 'Irn-Bru.'

The only person to even acknowledge me was the old lady who said, 'That's nice, dear', with a concerned look that suggested I should go home and take my medication.

Back to Michael. After getting over the initial shock of the sock situation, my mind went into overdrive, taking me to the image of him lying naked on a dark carpet, and noting that if he covered his face he would be camouflaged perfectly – save for the garish green socks. My bizarre brain then connected the dots between this and the fact that Michael is a pilot. Ha-ha, I thought, he is a flying carpet. That took me, a massive Disney nut, to Aladdin and his flying carpet, and then to the Genie, voiced wonderfully by Robin Williams.

Fortunately, I didn't shout anything out loud, as the situation was weird enough. Instead, as frequently happens, it did leave an echo in my brain that converted itself into a song. In Michael's presence, it became The Jean Genie by David Bowie, which I hummed throughout the appointment.

Michael's wax went without a hitch once he realised it wasn't going to be as painful as he had feared. What has bothered *me* to this day, is why was he only getting his cock and balls waxed? He never offered an explanation, and I didn't want to ask. It wasn't because he was putting on a wetsuit; for someone so hirsute that would be agonising. It wasn't to go on holiday

– people going on holiday are waxed to get a better tan – unless he was planning on covering everything except his testicles as he lay on the sun lounger. And I doubted it was for anything sexual, because if partner wasn't put off by the rest of the body hair, a little more would surely not matter.

Hubby didn't agree. He thought that Michael might enjoy glory holing, a term he had to explain to me, since I assumed it was a new slang term for a vagina. Apparently, a glory hole is a hole cut out at waist height in the side of a toilet cubicle. A man then puts his penis through the hole into the next cubicle and another man sucks him off. Seemingly, the excitement comes from the anonymity. The suckee can't see who is pleasuring him and the sucker can only see their cock. (I really hope this isn't where the saying, 'suck it and see,' comes from.)

I was a little concerned as to why hubby seemed to know so much about this. He assured me it was just common general knowledge, and was surprised I didn't know. After our conversation I found myself singing, Diana Ross's, I'm Coming Out.

'I know what you're doing, pack it in,' hubby said, annoyed.

Michael only came once, so I guess I will never know, but I will never be able to watch Aladdin again without thinking about that naked pilot in his socks.

CHAPTER THIRTEEN

Sally

LOVE'S YOUNG DREAM

I have clients of all ages. As far as I am concerned there is no prejudice when it comes to waxing, and I love the variety of chat this allows me to experience every day. I have people who remember the fifties clearly and some who weren't even about in the nineties. In the space of two minutes, from one client to the next, I can go from talking about Doris Day in Calamity Jane to tales of getting wasted on Jagerbombs in the Student Union.

For intimate waxing, though, I do draw the line at sixteen as a minimum age. I have waxed people who are younger, but only lower legs and armpits, and only when accompanied by a parent. This doesn't happen often, and it tends to be in extreme cases, where kids have been bullied for how hairy they are.

To be fair, intimate waxing for under-sixteens wasn't something I considered until I met Sally. She called to book in for a full Hollywood (all the pubic hair is removed), telling me this was going to be a first wax. It struck me as a little odd, as by the sound of her voice I would have placed her in her early forties. However, this wasn't unheard of, I do have clients who only began waxing in middle age, having tired of shaving. But she also sounded a little snooty, like a person who didn't do anything DIY, even her own downstairs grooming. Still, I always try not to jump to conclusions – I *have* been wrong before (just don't tell hubby I said that).

It was a glorious day, with the sun splitting the sky, when Sally arrived for her appointment. She rocked up in a red, convertible BMW, with private registration number, music blaring. She was the epitome of *look at me*. All hair and high heels, her outfit belied her true age, as did her figure and face, even with some obvious signs of a nip here and a tuck there. It was her neck that betrayed her. Once you get to a certain age, no amount of surgery can cover up the age of your neck, and therefore the rest of your body. On first sight I conservatively put her at forty-five, by no means old, but I imagined Sally would think it was.

She was accompanied by a mini-me, a much younger version, also all hair and high heels and teeth, but no obvious surgery. I placed her at about twenty-one.

And this was a prime example of why you shouldn't jump to conclusions; I was wrong on both counts. Sally was fifty-four, so all the effort she had clearly went to had paid off. Young Sally, or Lindsay, which was her name, was only fourteen.

Women amaze me. When we are young, we desperately try to look older, and when we are older, we pay a fortune to try and look younger. I think we are only truly happy, when we're so old we're more concerned about which internal organs are working properly, rather than the size of our crow's feet.

Lindsay was forged in her mother's image, and I wondered how much of that was through choice, and how much was down to Sally living vicariously through her teenage daughter. I imagined if she tried hard enough, she could convince herself that the admiring looks from young men were for her rather than her child. Either way, personality-wise the apple hadn't fallen far from the tree. Lindsay was every bit as obnoxious as her mother. If anything, she was worse, as she had no life experience which could have led to her shitty attitude. If nothing else, Sally had pushed at least one child into this world – and trust me, that can leave you feeling just a little entitled.

They waltzed into the waiting area as if they were the headline act at a music festival. I half-expected them to announce, 'We have arrived.' Instead, Sally looked around and grimaced as if she had stumbled into a junkie's squat.

'Lindsay is here for her wax, it's a Hollywood, I spoke to a woman on the phone about it. I assume it was you?' she shrilled.

No 'Hello'. No 'How are you?' Straight into business. My hackles were up immediately. I wanted to say, 'Well, given I am self-employed and work from home, who do you think it was you spoke to, you fucking moron? My live-in butler? And where might *she* live, in my three-bed semi-detached? In the Harry Potter room under the stairs?' But I didn't, because I have a business to run, and you can't call clients *fucking morons.* Even if they are.

Instead, I politely invited Lindsay through to the treatment room to fill out her consultation form, bearing in mind I was still estimating her age at twenty-one or twenty-two. Sally barged past and planted herself on the chair at the bottom of the bed. I intended to ask her to leave before the treatment started, but we never got that far. As I was inspecting Lindsay's completed form, I noted she had made a mistake with her date of birth.

'Sorry, hon, you've made a mistake with your date of birth here. I take it you are twenty-four, but this date puts you at fourteen,' I said as I handed the clip board back to her to amend the date.

'She is fourteen,' Supermum snapped at me, with a look that would make Medusa crumble.

For a second, I stared open mouthed at this dreadful woman. I must have looked like the idiot she clearly thought I was. I quickly composed myself and explained that unfortunately I would be unable to carry out the treatment, due to Lindsay's age. This did not go down well at all. Lindsay immediately rolled her eyes and fixed her mother with a look of, 'Fix this.'

Sally was apoplectic. 'I fail to see what the problem is. You are a waxer, now wax. This is how you make your money isn't it? Lindsay has something very important happening tomorrow and you are going to ruin it,' she seethed.

Something told me that Sally wasn't used to being told no. Curiosity got the better of me. I knew I wasn't going to treat her, but I really wanted to know what was so important that a fourteen-year-old child had to have a Hollywood wax.

In all honesty, I wish I'd never asked, as the answer just eroded my faith in humanity a little more.

'Lindsay is going to go all the way with her boyfriend tomorrow, and everything must be perfect,' she explained, as if this was the most normal thing in the world.

Lindsay's boyfriend was two years older and one of the most popular guys in school. The young lovebirds had been together for four weeks, and apparently if Lindsay didn't put out soon, she was going to lose him. This would, apparently, be social suicide, and if she wanted to reach the upper echelons of school society, she would have to open her legs. And *this* was the advice the child was getting from her mother! The woman meant to protect her and teach her what it means to be a strong independent woman. Er... Emmeline Pankhurst, anyone?

To say I was disgusted would be an understatement. Other than Mr Rapey, I have never had any reason to throw a client out of my treatment room. Until Sally. I let rip, I told her exactly what I thought of her, business be damned. I couldn't even blame Lindsay for her shitty attitude. Growing up with that woman must have been torture.

My words bounced off both of them. Sally clearly wasn't interested in my opinion of her parenting or what I thought of the impact on her child. As she got up to storm out, she informed me she would be leaving a dreadful review on Facebook, so that people would know how bad I was. This, even though I never actually waxed her or her daughter.

I said that was fine, just so long as she didn't mind me responding to explain how she was pimping out her fourteen-year-old daughter for popularity points.

Unsurprisingly, Sally never left a review.

Chapter Fourteen

Jeannie

Battle of the Bulge...

At seventy-six, Jeannie is one of my oldest clients. Without the assistance of her hearing aids, she is profoundly deaf; for reasons unknown, Jeannie usually chooses not to wear said hearing aids. As a result, she shouts absolutely everything she is saying, and she can't hear a word anyone says to her. Conversation is difficult, and giving her directions during a wax, nigh on impossible.

Hilariously, Jeannie tries to guess what you're saying to her, leading to some truly bizarre exchanges. On one occasion, I was telling her about my daughter receiving a certificate of merit from school. Jeannie advised me not to worry about it, just slather on some Germolene antiseptic cream. To this day, I have absolutely no idea what the hell she thought I had said.

One morning Jeannie arrived for an appointment and screamed her usual greeting, 'HELLO, LOVE,' right in my face. She watched my lips for a reply, and satisfied I was finished speaking, she bellowed, 'I'VE GOT A PROBLEM, LOVE.'

Yes, I replied mentally. You're as deaf as a post and won't wear your hearing aids, but this can't be news to you.

'I'VE GOT A BULGE,' she continued with gusto. 'DOWN THERE IN MY PANTS. I'VE TRIED TO PUSH IT BACK IN, BUT IT WON'T BUDGE.'

What Jeannie had was a vaginal prolapse, which I quickly ascertained when she got herself positioned on the bed. Now, I am no gynaecologist, so I can't offer a professional diagnosis, but I can tell when someone's insides are hanging out of their fanny. Rather than contact her GP, or go up to the hospital, Jeannie had literally been battling to push her innards back in. Truly the most bizarre battle of the bulge I have ever heard of.

In a way I suppose it's admirable, and probably a generational thing, not wanting to put undue stress on the National Health System. On the flip side, I've seen people in their early twenties sitting in A&E with nothing more than a hangover. But when you are literally turning inside out, you need to get to a medical professional. Trying to shove it back up with the handle of a broom isn't going to cut it.

I tried to explain this to Jeannie and found myself repeatedly screaming, 'YOU HAVE A VAGINAL PROLAPSE,' into the face of a bewildered old woman. I was very conscious that if the neighbours overheard me, they might think this a case of a wax gone seriously wrong. I could just imagine Sylvie talking to Liz:

'Did you hear that Mona ripped someone's womb out when she was waxing her lady garden?'

'No. Really?'

'Yep, I heard it myself through the window. She must have put the wax too far up and ripped the whole lot right out.'

Unfortunately, I couldn't even give Jeannie a written explanation to tell her to seek medical assistance, because she had forgotten her reading glasses. Eventually, I decided to send her home with a note that she could read later.

Whether or not the neighbours heard me screaming I don't know, but I suddenly became aware that *someone* had. I had no idea that hubby was in his office, he must have come in just after Jeannie arrived and was screaming hello at me.

I could hear his chair creaking next door, as it struggled with his mammoth bulk. I imagined that the gas cylinder, which controls the height adjustment, was under such immense pressure that it could blow at any moment. You know you're too fat when furniture starts to give up on you. Even worse, as the years went by, he had become so fat that between his gut and the pube ringlets, you could barely make out his penis. With just the head peeking out it looked like a fat clitoris. In fact, with his ample bosom, and close-cropped hair, he made a more than passable lesbian.

I kept thinking he would have his magazine moment. You know, when you see those before and after stories in women's magazines, when people lose three quarters of their body weight? In the accompanying photographs they stand proudly in one leg of their old trousers, holding the waist band out to the side, to display how much weight they have lost. Each person has their own special reason for what motivated them to lose weight: maybe they saw pictures of themselves at a family wedding and realised that they were bigger than all the bridesmaids combined. Or perhaps they got trapped in the bath and had to be rescued by the fire service.

So far, nothing had motivated hubby to his magazine moment, even when his fat arse sank a boat. That's right, he sank a boat with nothing other than his own bulk. He would have been a real asset during the Battle of Trafalgar.

The incident happened at a theme park not far from us. It was a beautiful summer's day, and as the kids were young, we spent it on the family friendly rides, and at the petting zoo. Towards the end of the day hubby decided to take our daughter on the barrel ride. Yes, I know a theme park barrel isn't quite the same as a boat, but it was designed to be buoyant with up to eight adults in it.

If you are unfamiliar with the barrel ride, then let me explain. Passengers embark from a platform at the start of the ride as the barrels move slowly along a conveyor belt adjacent to the platform. At the end of the belt each barrel gently drops into the water and slowly bobs along. It continues its journey along a winding concourse, until returning to the platform, allowing the passengers to disembark. Everybody has a lovely time and leaves thoroughly relaxed.

Apart from The Incredible Bulk. He took his seat in the barrel and directed our eldest child to sit opposite. In his mind that must have been an even weight distribution – even though he regularly ate sandwiches bigger than her. They trundled slowly along the belt and dropped into the water like an elephant falling out of a tree house. The base of the barrel at hubby's side found the bottom of the fibreglass concourse, and that's where it stayed. No gentle bobbing along, enjoying the evening sun, instead a dead stop and an increasing sense of panic. Three barrels of excited children were behind him. One, two, three, they hit his barrel with a thud and caused gridlock; not an inch was given.

Options were limited. The concourse was on legs, several feet in the air, so even if he could launch himself from the sunken vessel, hubby would probably break a limb. Even a three-foot drop can prove deadly for the clinically obese. Repositioning himself in the centre of the barrel had a limited effect, just grounding it on a more even keel. It also meant he had to adopt a squatting position, something he usually reserved for retrieving bounty from the vending machine at the swimming pool. (I hasten to add he never swam at the pool, just spectated and snacked.)

He eventually found that by levelling the barrel, he could grab the sides of the concourse and pull the stricken vessel along. Even for a regular gym goer this would have been quite a workout – dragging a dead weight a few hundred yards, in a squatting position is not easy, and particularly so when you are so fat you can't see your own feet, even when lying down.

I don't know what gave him strength that day, possibly the laughter of the children in the barrels behind him echoing in his ears. Whatever it was, he did it, and disembarked sweaty and breathless.

This is it, I thought at the time: hubby's magazine moment. If anything was going to motivate him, surely it would be public humiliation. As he made his way towards me, I gave him my best, 'It's okay we can fix this', look, and prepared to mitigate his embarrassment.

'It could happen to anybody', was a good phrase to use, I thought, or, 'I think that you got a defective one.' I'd blame the equipment; men are always doing that.

I shouldn't have concerned myself. The first thing hubby said was, 'I'm peckish, can we grab a burger?'

Seriously, the man was literally a laughing stock and all he could think about was feeding the belly that caused the issue. A little part of me was jealous, to be honest. I wished I had that lack of self-awareness.

Later, in the car on the way home, he asked me if I saw the German family that had been laughing at him. Finally, I thought, it had sunk in (pardon the pun), and he realised it was time to make a lifestyle change. I was intrigued as to why a German family laughing at him proved to be the catalyst. I wondered if hubby was perhaps a little xenophobic and I had never picked up on it.

'Yeah, there was a German family standing laughing hysterically, and the dad was filming me,' he explained.

I started to get a little angry. Yes, he was a chubster, but he was my chubster, and those bloody Germans were documenting his misfortune. I had to fight the urge to go back and find them to give them a piece of my mind.

'I hope they get that film out and watch it every now and again to give themselves a laugh,' hubby said chuckling. 'It must have looked so funny, a big fat guy having to pull himself round whilst squatting like a gorilla.'

The man spoke with no ego at all. This is part of the reason I love him so much, he likes to find the funny just as much as I do – even if he is the butt of the joke. I overheard him once, telling the kids he doesn't mind if people are laughing with him or at him. So long as they are laughing, he's happy.

Once Jeannie had left with her note, I popped into his office to explain what had happened. He winced as I told him about her predicament and he commented how fortunate he was to be a man, as he couldn't cope with such a fate. His face was a picture when I explained how men can suffer from rectal prolapse. It's quite common in obese people, I told him, as they tend to suffer from constipation, which can be a major factor in your arse falling out.

That turned out to be his magazine moment. The look of horror on his face as he wrestled with the idea of shitting his own arse out was hilarious. Within a year he lost 105lbs and regularly monitored his bowel movements.

As for Jeannie, she underwent surgery, and everything was put back in its correct place.

Both successfully battled very different bulges, and I can happily tell you at the time of writing, both Jeannie's lady garden and hubby's sphincter are suitably tight.

Chapter Fifteen

Alix

Pulling the plug...

Working at the business end of multiple clients a day takes a certain degree of fortitude. This is particularly so, when personal hygiene seems to be such a subjective thing.

Call me crazy, but I am a firm believer in taking a shower at least once a day, and if I am ever going to be showing someone my vagina and butthole, particularly in a scheduled appointment, I like to make sure the area is spic and span. Don't get me wrong, there are instances a little more spontaneous than a wax or a gynaecology appointment – I'm thinking romantic relations, not flashing in the local park – where you may unveil your nether regions with scant regard for freshness, but for some people, wiping after going to the toilet would appear to be too much effort, let alone the luxury of applying soap and water. This can lead to quite an assault on the senses.

The first casualty in the attack is the nose, as the smell tends to hit first. Just as we all have our own DNA sequence and fingerprints, we also have our own personal aroma – you know what I'm talking about. At some point we have all found ourselves lying in bed, unwashed for two or three days, maybe due to illness or maybe abject laziness over the Christmas holidays. Eventually you pull the duvet up over your head and it catches you, your own unique smell. Initially you might gag a little at the warm stench, but quickly you accept it and let it envelop you. We're all happy to bask in our own stink on occasion.

When you need to deal with other people's smell, it's a whole different ball game. There are plenty of occupations where you need to tolerate others' odours to varying degrees. Taxi drivers let strangers in to the close confines of their vehicle, so even the slightest hint of B.O. becomes obvious. Hairdressers need to stand directly over their customer as they work, and if they haven't washed their hair it can be a whiffy affair. Chiropodists spend their day with their face at client's feet, and we all know how cheesy that could be.

I'm sure you would agree, though, that none of these compare to having your face up close and personal with an unwashed asshole. The range of smells runs the full spectrum from barely noticeable, to 'I think something has died in here'. It is not unheard of, after a whiffy client, for my treatment room to smell like a poorly-cleaned pet shop on a hot summer's day.

The second victim of the assault is the eyes. They are more of a reluctant victim, as the nose has sent them a stern warning, 'Don't look, don't look. Anything smelling as bad as this must look fucking awful.' Of course, you need to look, even when the nose is making the eyes water to try and protect them from the coming onslaught. And that's when you see the shit. The dried-in shit, matted to the hair.

Did you know that hot wax won't stick to shit? So the shit needs to be cleaned off. A pre-wax cleanse is always carried out on any area about to be waxed, so while it is not a massive inconvenience, you are still cleaning excrement from an adult human's bum. I didn't even have to do that for my kids after they started primary school.

The sense of taste doesn't suffer the same onslaught as the nose and eyes, but it is affected by the worst of it. There are smells that are so bad you can taste them in your mouth, and they leave you unable to eat for hours afterwards.

The sense of touch is spared thanks to the wonder of latex gloves. Touch is oblivious to what's going on, protected as it is by its waterproof coat. Hearing tends to be off the hook, as well, unless the offender adjusts themselves on the bed and produces an involuntary squelch.

As an intimate waxer you need to become adept at not only tolerating the full gambit of aromas, but also pretending to the client the smell doesn't even exist.

You could be forgiven for forming a picture of the type of client you imagine is particularly odorous – and I wager you'd be wrong. You may be thinking of someone a little dishevelled, hair unkempt with food-stained clothes. And while there are some like that, you might be surprised that an example of my worst offenders is easily one of the most beautiful young women I have ever met. She spends a fortune every month on her hair and nails, hours a week on applying make-up and then removing it, carrying out a strict skin care regime religiously. Her wardrobe is immaculate and fake tan is applied regularly for that sun-kissed look without the skin damage. She visits the gym three days a week to maintain her envious figure. Even without all of it she is a natural beauty. Wherever she goes men fall at her feet. She has her pick of the guys.

I can't imagine they would be quite so keen, if they saw the amount of dried-in crap I have had to clean off her ass in the last few years. Don't get me wrong, she is a lovely girl, and I'm very fond of her, but there is no reason to turn up for a wax with an unwiped bum.

Even though I have built up a particularly strong constitution over the years, there was one incident in my treatment room that left me gagging.

Alix is one of my younger clients, in her early twenties, and a self-proclaimed party animal. I can't schedule her appointments for the weekend as she is either drunk or hungover. Alcohol thins the blood and makes the client more sensitive to pain, so usually I book her in for a Wednesday, to allow her body time to recover.

On one occasion, Alix asked for a Monday appointment because she was going on holiday on the Wednesday. I didn't see a problem with that; I assumed she would be taking it easy the weekend before her holiday. When she turned up for her appointment she seemed as fresh as a daisy and full of excitement for her vacation. And just to make it clear, Alix had never turned up anything other than clean as a whistle down below. She was not a poopy pants, as the kids used to call it when they were toilet training.

Her appointment was going perfectly normally, and the chat was flowing. She was off to Thailand to go scuba diving with her boyfriend, and we were blethering away about all the cool stuff she had planned for the trip.

Positioned on all fours I applied the wax to her butt hole and waited for it to set. But what Alix had failed to tell me was that she had been pissed all weekend, drinking right through to the early hours of Monday morning. Her stomach was churning, and when she arrived for her wax, she already had an overwhelming need to empty her bowels. I didn't find out any of this information until later.

As I pulled the wax from her butt it was like pulling the plug from a bath, and she violently shat all over me and the treatment room. Like a faecal pressure washer, she sprayed a weekend's worth of booze and takeaway curry all over my white walls.

It was overwhelming. I could feel the warmth of the liquid shit as it seeped through my clothes to my skin. The smell hit me like a sledgehammer and I gagged, dry retching.

I could hear Alix, simultaneously laughing and crying, both at the ridiculousness of it all and the sheer embarrassment. Fortunately, it happened at the end of her wax, as although I pride myself on providing a professional service, no matter what the obstacle, even I draw the line at working in a shit-painted room.

When I told hubby about it later, he thought it was hilarious. Like most men, he finds anything poo-based very humorous, which I think is some form of universal male arrested development. I have to warn him every time we go to a party, not to tell the story about the time he shat himself on his paper round when he was fourteen. It was due to him eating nine bowls of bran flakes the night before. Who does that? Nobody eats nine bowls of bran flakes, not even pensioners.

Once he stopped laughing, I wiped the smile off his face by telling him he could go out and clean up the workroom and repaint the walls. He tried to remonstrate, but I quickly reminded him that I had pushed two human beings into this world from my vagina. This is an argument I intend to use until one of us is dead, and it will always be a winner. Well, unless he pushes an actual person out of his penis, but I'm not holding my breath.

Understandably, Alix was mortified, and she called round with a bottle of Pinot for me before she left for Thailand. I appreciated it, but there was really no need; once you've had kids, getting shat on just becomes a part of life.

Chapter Sixteen

Angela

Filthy girl...

Angela, like many others, started as a client but became a friend. Our lives mirror, the similarities are uncanny. We are the same age, from a similar background, and are married with two kids, albeit she has two boys. Angela is a hairdresser, so she also removes hair from people for a living.

Most importantly she likes to laugh, loudly and often. You hear Angela long before you see her, her guffaws are more like a foghorn than a laugh. Nothing is off limits either, which I love.

On one occasion she couldn't wait to get into my treatment room to tell me about something she'd done. Her lips curled into a devilish grin, her shoulders raised like a naughty schoolgirl and she could barely contain herself as she told me what had happened the night before.

The kids were in bed and Angela and Terry had decided to indulge in a rare night of passion, or what passes for passion with kids in the house. Nonetheless, they were getting down to sexy time and Terry was offering up his usual patter: 'You like that, don't you?' and, 'You're a naughty girl, aren't you?' Angela, like most women, plays her part with the expected replies: 'Ooh yeah, baby, I love it. You're the best,' and, 'I'm such a naughty girl and I need you to punish me,' or words to that effect. Because if she were to be honest, it would somewhat kill the moment: 'No, I don't like that actually. Clawing at my tit like a bear trying to get honey from a beehive, isn't really doing it for me I'm afraid.' That just doesn't flow as part of sexy time, nor does, 'Yeah, I've been a really naughty girl. I forgot to put fabric softener in with the laundry detergent, and now your work shirts are going to be scratchy.'

But Angela knows her role and plays along – except for the one phrase, well, two words, she will not tolerate in the bedroom. It's 'juicy pussy' and it turns her stomach. And for some reason Terry still insists on throwing it in every now and again. Like that night.

Whilst laid on his back with Angela straddling him cowgirl style, he hit out with,

'Oh, baby that's it. Give me that juicy pussy.'

Angela slapped him hard on the chest and threw him a look to wither the toughest of men.

Choosing to ignore the warning shot, Terry tried,

'Oh yes work it. Work that juicy pussy.'

Just a little tip for you gentlemen out there, never piss a woman off when you have your penis inside her. Trust me, it is way worse than pissing her off when you don't have your penis inside her. Angela told me she couldn't remember ever being so angry as she was right then. Sexy time was well and truly over, for her, anyway. Terry didn't realise that yet.

Angela stayed calm and repositioned herself into a reverse cowgirl, meaning she was still on top but facing away from Terry. Like most working mums, Angela had desperately needed the toilet since long before the kids had been put to bed (it's just one of the things busy mums regularly put off until everything else is done) and as she was slowly riding up and down on Terry, her bowels were full. She waited until she was halfway on the down stroke – and she shat all over him.

'How's that for a juicy pussy?' she said as she took herself through to the en-suite to get cleaned up.

Apparently, Terry was still staring down at the massive shit his wife had just taken on his stomach as she left the room to go and watch her soaps.

At this stage, I feel I must apologise for the level of shit my stories contain. It does seem to be a disproportionate amount for one human in their day to day life, but as I like to remind anyone who starts to get an over inflated sense of self-worth, none of us is anything but a smart ape. Neither have we evolved much from the shit-slinging chimps you see in the zoo. I'm sure you, too, have your own stories that revolve around faecal matter, though admittedly, a wife shitting on her husband, for telling her she had a juicy pussy, is a little out there even for me.

As usual, Amanda and I fell about laughing. I couldn't help but feel a little sorry for Terry but I'm sure he heard the message loud and clear.

And smelled it too.

Chapter Seventeen

Jim and Marjorie

Vegging out...

They say that wisdom comes with age. With that in mind, my clients Jim and Marjorie, combined, come with a lot of wisdom. Marjorie is eighty-one, and Jim, the old cradle snatcher, is ninety. And they are very much my favourite couple; a reminder of times gone by, when women were demure and men were gentlemen; before binge drinking and late-night kebabs; when reality TV star was not a profession, and people didn't share their entire lives on social media.

I doubt very much Jim ever uttered the phrase 'juicy pussy', for example, and I am almost certain Marjorie never curled one out on his stomach. (And I promise their story does not involve anyone shitting on themselves, or on others. It is, like Jim and Marjorie, far more pedestrian.)

Marjorie comes to me for an upper lip and chin wax, a super quick treatment. However, I always allow for an appointment time at least twice as long, partly because they are both quite slow, but mostly because I love a blether with them. I get a warm feeling inside every time I hear Jim refer to his wife as, 'my darling', and my belly flutters when I see the way that they look at each other. They had never been able to have children, they tried, but medical science at the time was nowhere near advanced enough to pinpoint the problem, so they have always been each other's world. Even more so since Jim retired and they could spend every minute together.

He always attends every appointment she has, taking her arm as they walk up the garden path, opening the door for her, and helping her up on to the treatment bed. He then sits dutifully at the back of the room, whilst I work my magic.

I love to listen to tales of their lives together, which are offered along with advice on how to make a marriage work. On the face of it, much of the advice may seem outdated, and a little flowery, but it is sound.

It boils down to respect and remembering what you loved about the person when you agreed to spend your life with them. Spending time with Marjorie and Jim is like pressing pause on hectic, modern-day life.

During one of Marjorie's first appointments with me, Jim let slip it was her birthday. I felt terrible, had I known in advance I would have got her a card and gift, even though the cost would have far outweighed the price of her treatment. Caught on the hop, I told Marjorie her treatment was on me as it was her birthday and apologised it was such a meagre offering for her big day. Both seemed overly impressed with my offer, given it only saved them a few pounds. I put it down to a generation thing, particularly their remembering rationing first hand. After having survived one of the most desolate times in recent British history, you must appreciate the smallest of gestures.

Then it became clear, at Marjorie's next appointment, there had been a slight misunderstanding.

Arriving bang on time – Jim was not a fan of tardiness – Marjorie was swinging a bulging carrier bag.

'This is for you,' she said, thrusting the bag towards me.

I opened it to find an inordinate amount of runner beans. Just a ridiculous amount, far more than a family of four could get through.

'Oh, how lovely,' I managed, trying to mask my confusion. I knew Jim was a very keen gardener, preferring to grow as much as he could of the fruit and veg they consumed. A big fan of seasonal food, he continues to regularly express his dismay at the year-round produce provided by the supermarkets. Importing fresh food from South America does not sit at all well with him.

'We were both so touched with your offer of not charging me for my waxing that we felt it would be rude to turn up empty-handed,' Marjorie explained.

Whoops. It appeared my free birthday wax had been misinterpreted as never charging her again. Ordinarily, this would have been nothing more than mildly awkward for me. Had it been anyone else, I would have simply corrected them and cleared up any confusion – problem solved.

But as they were both so lovely, and the treatment so inexpensive, I found myself playing along – and have been paid in vegetables ever since. To my knowledge, I am the only waxer in the 21st century to be paid in carrots, turnips, peas, marrows, tomatoes, raspberries, strawberries, and rhubarb. It's like some bartering service from the Middle Ages, akin to the town's blacksmith exchanging work for a goat.

The whole thing was so sweet, especially as each bag of produce came with some lovely recipe suggestions from Marjorie; the kind of home-cooked meals that would have been written down and passed down the generations, if they had kids. So, I felt honoured to be receiving something that had been lovingly grown, through time and effort, and passed on, with wisdom and experience. They would have made wonderful grandparents.

It did make it quite tricky, though, as I was unsure how to declare vegetable earnings on my tax return. I asked hubby about it, given his area of expertise, but he found the whole situation so hilarious, that any time I brought the subject up he couldn't stop himself from laughing. And I wouldn't have been that bothered, had it not been that a short while after, I found out he had allowed one of his clients to pay him in shortbread. For two years. At *his* bloody suggestion.

As you know from the sunken barrel incident, hubby is a glutton who has no control over his gut. This has led to many heated discussions in our house about his diet, which ultimately means he participates in a lot of secret eating. I only discovered his sweet deceit when I went into his office, looking for a pen, and found an entire drawer of home-made shortbread. This explained a lot, as his biscuit purchases, unlike his weight, had dropped massively in the weekly shop. His change in shopping habits coincided with a new client two years previously, who baked cakes and biscuits to order. Apparently, what began as a small venture, a supplement on the side of her B&B, had become a nice little earner. With increasing business and decreasing time, the woman contacted hubby to take on her bookkeeping. Meeting her for the first time, he was offered a cup of tea and a piece of shortbread. After one piece, he embarrassed himself by asking to be paid in shortbread. Actual shortbread. Not money. I couldn't believe it when he told me.

To him, it was perfect. For two whole years, on the surface of it, it appeared he was trying to control his biscuit consumption, yet he was hiding his stash of sweet treats to eat in secret.

Some wives need to worry about their husband having a coke habit, with a secret drug dealer in their contacts. I had to worry about a sugar addict with a secret shortbread dealer. I won't lie, though, once I tried the shortbread I let him off with it. It is bloody amazing – and now is kept in the house for everyone to share.

Chapter Eighteen

Mona's Top Three

Excuses, Excuses, Excuses...

Any business or organisation which operates on an appointment system is bound to be affected by no-shows, and latecomers. Just look on the wall the next time you are in the waiting room at your doctor's surgery, where there is, no doubt, a notice highlighting the number of missed appointments that month.

Waxing is no different and it is probably the most frustrating part of my job. Don't get me wrong, most of my clients are great. They never miss an appointment and they always show up on time. I do, however, have a select group who are repeat offenders, either turning up consistently late or not at all.

Like most salons I have a cancellation policy. For any cancellations made within 24 hours of the appointment, or appointments missed altogether, I reserve the right to charge payment in full.

Unlike most salons, I can rarely bring myself to enforce this policy, mostly because I get on so well with my clients, but also because it doesn't seem so bad as I pretty much work from home.

Nevertheless, it does piss me off when people turn up late, or not at all, as it throws my whole day off. Over the years I have heard pretty much every excuse imaginable, diarrhoea being the most common. People assume you'll be grateful they are not presenting their arse to you when it has been spraying liquid shit. So much so, they think you wouldn't doubt them. To a waxer saying you have a runny bum is like telling the stereotypical male boss that you can't come in because you have 'women's problems.' It might work but nobody believes you.

Fortunately, some people really raise the bar when it comes to excuses. For your enjoyment I have compiled Mona's Top Three Excuses. Each of these excuses have honestly been offered to me by clients, and far be it for me to doubt anyone's honesty, but in my opinion two of these are genuine reasons and the other one is, well, horse shit. I'll let you make up your own mind which is which.

Like Top of the Pops I shall give you them in ascending order, finishing with my favourite.

In third place we have Anne, without doubt the most prolific of excuse givers. When it comes to timekeeping Anne is quite frankly, a shambles. In over six years she has never been on time for an appointment. And to make matters worse, she has a fifty-five per cent no-show rate. The only reason I still book her in is so I can hear her next excuse. Some are better than others, often she makes no creative effort whatsoever. She has buried her gran seven times already – the same gran she has just come back from the Lake District with.

Unbelievably, Anne holds down a full-time, hugely responsible job, as a paramedic. I can't imagine what her stats are on fatalities. I just hope her loss rate isn't as high as her no shows with me.

I get on well with Anne even though she frustrates the hell out of me and she is categorically not winning at being an adult. In her forties and single, she lives alone with her cat, Henry. Her flat constantly looks like it has been burgled and despite her medical background, she lives off junk food. A conservative estimate would put her at least five stone overweight.

This would all be fine if she was happy, but she's not. Every appointment is filled with her bitching about not being able to find a man and how she needs to sort her weight. I try to sympathise but after the tenth time of hearing it, tend to lose patience.

After turning up late, again, for a Saturday morning appointment she hit me with her best excuse ever. It was already ten minutes into her twenty-minute appointment when she turned up, sobbing. I mean proper chest-heaving sobbing. Tears streaked her face and her eyes were bright red.

I put my arm around her and bundled her into my treatment room, where I sat her down. I rubbed her shoulder, soothing her as best I could, to try and get her breathing under control. I hadn't seen anyone that upset since my friend Karen found out Take That were splitting up in 1996. I thought her gran was dead for sure this time and that she felt guilty for tempting fate.

It took a full two minutes to calm her down enough to get her to speak.

'Anne what's wrong, how can I help you?' I asked her.

Breathing in hard, like a toddler at the end of a tantrum, she just about managed to compose herself.

'It's Henry,' she blurted. 'I think he has AIDS.'

She wailed uncontrollably as I tried desperately to process what she had just told me.

'What do you mean? You think your cat has AIDS?' I was genuinely confused.

'Yes. I think he has AIDS. What am I going to do?' she cried.

It took every fibre of my being to not shout, 'And how the fuck does that make you late for your waxing appointment?'

But that would be an insensitive thing to do, even in the face of such a ludicrous excuse. Instead, my mind wandered to how poor Henry could possibly have contracted AIDS. Images of him in a back alley shooting up heroin using a shared needle flooded my brain. Perhaps he had taken to turning tricks to fund his Whiskas habit. How many cans of Whiskas can a cat have a day before it becomes a problem? Was he hanging about the park with the strays, eating straight from the tin with his paw? My mind raced with possibilities.

'What do you mean, you think he has AIDS?' I repeated.

'Well, I was just looking at him this morning and I thought he looked a little off. I picked him up and held him, staring into his eyes, and I just sensed from him that he has AIDS. I was so upset I couldn't even get dressed for an hour, I just sat and cried.'

Just to clarify, Anne didn't think that Henry had Feline Immunodeficiency Virus, or FIV, also known as cat AIDS.

Fun fact, FIV is the only non-primate lentivirus to cause an AIDS-like syndrome but is not typically lethal to cats. I'm not just a waxer you know, I'm also a font of knowledge. No, she had diagnosed Henry with actual human AIDS, which, in case you didn't know, is impossible.

This woman is an actual medical professional. People's lives are in her hands every day – and she is genuinely mad. I don't know if I have a duty of care to inform somebody at the NHS.

What do you say, though? I would have to be a pretty hard-faced bitch to tell her what I was thinking, which was, 'You mad bastard, of course your cat doesn't have AIDS, now pull yourself together and get your knickers off, I'm fifteen minutes behind as it is.' Instead, I found myself comforting her, and even offered to accompany her to the vets to get a blood test done on her cat. I couldn't even be angry. Anybody putting that much effort into such a half-arsed excuse gets a walk, as far as I am concerned.

For all you animal lovers out there, rest assured that Henry is AIDS free and living a happy life. You certainly won't see Channel 4 doing a Supervet special on him anytime soon.

In second place we have Kerry, one of my annoyingly young and beautiful clients. Kerry is very much a 'live in the moment' kind of girl, her impulsive nature frequently getting her into trouble. She is not the most reliable of clients in terms of timekeeping, but to be fair, she rarely misses an appointment and if she does it is usually due to illness.

I awoke one day to find a voicemail on my mobile, left by Kerry at about three in the morning. She had phoned from the toilet of a twenty-four-hour supermarket, clearly a little worse for wear and in her message she painted a vivid picture of her situation. Apologising profusely, in the way that only drunk people do, she was most upset that she was going to have to cancel her waxing appointment for later that morning.

Kerry and her friends had been on an impromptu night out in their home town and ended their night in the local nightclub, where it just so happened a well-known reality TV star was doing a personal appearance.

In the interest of discretion, I won't divulge who he was but in the age of reality TV stars he is a household name. Given her beauty and gym toned body, it is no surprise that Kerry caught his eye, and he made it clear that he would like to give her a *personal* personal appearance. If you know what I mean.

As I am over a certain age I don't really class these types of celebs as properly famous. But apparently, amongst the young folks, bedding a reality star would be the equivalent of shagging a rock star back in the day. (I imagine being intimate with any of The Rolling Stones would be like wrestling with someone's grandfather, but to each their own.)

Had the gentleman in question not been a 'personality', he would have had no chance with Kerry. Looks wise, he was punching way above his weight.

Anyway, after fulfilling his contractual duties at the club, Mr X suggested his driver take them back to his hotel. It was at this point Kerry realised she hadn't gone out that night planning to hook up with anybody and, obviously, with a wax appointment in just a few hours, her va-jay-jay wasn't looking as sharp as the rest of her.

So on the way back to the hotel Kerry asked the driver to stop at a twenty-four-hour supermarket, under the pretence that she needed the bathroom. Once in, she quickly bought razors and shaving gel, and nipped to the loo. That was why she was standing on one leg, the other propped up on the sink, shaving her fanny in front of the mirror. As outgoing as she is, shaving her vagina in the communal area of a public toilet in a supermarket was extreme and fortunately, nobody came in and witnessed her impromptu de-fuzzing.

If ever you needed proof that women excel at multi-tasking, imagine the skill needed to shave your own fanny when drunk, whilst still dressed and simultaneously phoning your waxing therapist to cancel your appointment. That kind of skill could get you through to the live rounds of Britain's Got Talent.

I couldn't even be angry at her for missing her wax, especially as she filled me in on all the juicy details a few weeks later. It turned out in 'reality' he wasn't such a *big* star after all.

Taking gold in first place of my all-time favourite excuses is Gary, who despite taking top spot has only ever been late once.

Gary is a police officer and one of the most straitlaced people I have ever met. As such, his timekeeping is impeccable, which is why it was such a shock when he didn't arrive on time one morning. Hubby is also a stickler for being on time, to the point of being annoying, he would rather turn up an hour early and wait, than be even a minute late. The problem with excellent timekeepers is that when they are late, you assume the worst. My other half was seven minutes late for dinner once and I seriously considered phoning around the local hospitals.

When Gary didn't turn up, of course I assumed the worst and thought he had been killed in the line of duty. Ultra-pessimism is one of my more negative personality traits, which I work hard to stay on top of. When I hear a noise in the house at night I automatically think, 'burglar'. Hubby hears the same noise and writes it off as, 'just the house talking'. Once he is in bed you could walk an elephant through the downstairs, and he would dismiss it as a 'house noise'. Mostly so he doesn't have to get back out of bed.

Gary arrived about ten minutes late. He had come straight from work, delayed because they had to attend a call shortly before their shift finished. It was a domestic between a husband and wife, and Gary and his partner were the first to the scene. They were met at the door by the wife, with a face like thunder, who led them into the living room. There they found the husband lying on the floor, his face covered by his hands, blood noticeably pouring from his nose.

After sitting him up against the couch, it was clear he had a couple of shiners, as well, his eyes badly swollen. The wife – let's call her Nora – had taken a seat and was lighting a cigarette, muttering under her breath. Gary tended to the husband – let's call him Barry – as his partner spoke to her to find out what had happened. Nora explained she had found messages on Barry's phone from another woman, some of which suggested he had been unfaithful. Nora confronted him with the evidence. Barry strenuously denied any wrongdoing, which enraged her as she felt he was trying to make a fool of her. She grabbed for the first thing she could reach on her bedside unit and lunged at him. Swinging wildly, she missed, and he fled downstairs with Nora in hot pursuit. Upon reaching the living room he turned to face her, and her second swing connected with his nose with such a force he was knocked on his arse.

Gary asked Nora what she had done with the weapon, and she pointed behind the couch, where she had thrown it. Looking over the back of the sofa Gary discovered an eight-inch dildo with a realistic ball-sack.

Explaining to Nora, that as she had used a weapon to assault Barry, she would need to be arrested for GBH, Gary did not expect her reply.

'He's fucking lucky I didn't grab my Black Destroyer, or you would be arresting me for attempted murder,' Nora fumed.

I had to Google this, so let me save you the time. A Black Destroyer is a 16" dildo (you can only insert 13", though, due to the balls) which has a suction cup for your convenience. Handy, because at 2.1 kilogrammes, it is rather weighty. Incidentally, if you do like a good laugh, go on Amazon and read the reviews for the Black Destroyer. I have just wasted an afternoon reading reviews for sex toys (with no intention of buying) and it has reaffirmed to me, just how crazy human beings are.

I found the whole scenario way more amusing than Gary did, particularly when I pointed out that they had both let their dicks get them into trouble.

I later found out the charges against Nora were dropped as Barry said he would refuse to testify. I can't imagine many men would stand up in court and admit to being laid out by a cock to the face from their wife.

So there you have it, my three favourite excuses.

And if I could offer you some advice on cancelling an appointment at short notice, without a valid reason, make your excuse as outlandish as you can. You are going to piss someone off, anyway, so you might as well give them a laugh. Why not try telling them that you think your budgie has syphilis?

CHAPTER NINETEEN

Arthur

SHOW ME...

I suppose when you do any job for long enough you become numb to it. A&E doctors must become oblivious to the blood and gore and just get on with the task at hand. Stand-up comedians must get so sick of hearing their own jokes every night, that there will be no humour left in them. (The jokes that is, not the comedians.)

For me, it's fannies and balls. If the average person were to go to work and be confronted with a pair of hairy balls they would probably be quite shocked and I'm almost certain Human Resources would get involved and somebody would be sent on a course about workplace etiquette. However, as I spend all day with people who willingly whip their underpants off to present me with their genitals, I begin to think that this is the norm – and sometimes forget that not everybody agrees.

Do you know who doesn't think this is the norm? Hubby's clients. As well as dealing with small businesses he also provides financial advice to individuals looking to invest their savings. These tend to be older people and many of them are a little stuffy. Usually he goes to their home, a service which many of them appreciate, but there are a few who prefer to come to him and occasionally I cross paths with them.

Arthur is one such person, who I have met on a couple of occasions. A retired school teacher, he inherited some money when his mother died. When I say 'some' money, I mean a nice amount but in no way a lottery win, but by the frequency with which he visits hubby to check on his investments you would think he was Lord Alan Sugar.

I get the feeling he thinks hubby is some sort of Nick Leeson character, he who famously brought down Barings Bank with his rogue trading. Unlike Leeson, though, hubby doesn't have access to billions of pounds, and in no way is he involved in speculative trading. Most of Arthur's money is in ISAs, something which he readily tells anybody he meets, largely because he is one of the most boring humans on the planet.

That's why I was surprised when I heard him, as he was leaving one day, discussing his recent vasectomy operation. Why a man of his age would be getting a vasectomy, I did not know. Especially when you see his wife – a terrifying woman, both in appearance and personality, and with scant regard to personal hygiene. Even with a bottle of Viagra and a strong tailwind I couldn't imagine Arthur maintaining an erection. The odour alone could wilt the most amorous of men.

Arthur was bemoaning how swollen his testicles were, so large, apparently, that he struggled to get his pants on. He was clearly unaware that I was in my treatment room and could hear everything he was saying and I took this as my cue to involve myself in the conversation. Now, I can't offer any explanation for what I did next and hubby has never forgiven me for it but stepping into the waiting room, I opened with, 'Let me see them.'

Yep, I asked a man in his late sixties, who was in to see my husband for financial advice, to show me his balls. I had confused the nature of my job and the openness of my clients, with general reality. In the moment I forgot that it isn't the norm for people to show you their genitals while you are at work. I did it, I think, because he was in my workplace. I have certainly never done it anywhere else. I have never gone into Greggs and said, 'Two sausage rolls please, and give us a glance of your fanny while you're at it.'

Arthur looked at me with a level of contempt that suggested I had just pissed in his hat. (I didn't piss in his hat, but hubby said I may as well have.) Worse still, I failed to pick up on Arthur's reluctance to show me his balls and tried to cajole him into dropping his trousers. It was purely curiosity peaking my interest – in no way was it an attempt to have a ménage-a-trois with my husband and a pensioner – and I thought it would be hilarious to see some massive balls.

Arthur was quickly ushered out by hubby. I say quickly, it was more of a slow waddle, but it can't be easy walking with massive balls. After Arthur left, the ensuing argument was probably in the top three of our epic fallouts. I very quickly conceded that it was possibly inappropriate of me to have asked one of my husband's clients to show me his testicles. Hubby, however, refused to accept my theory as to why *he* was being such a prude, which was due to an unfortunate experience of his own, twenty years earlier.

Now, I am fully aware that at no point was hubby's prudishness in question during this scenario, but I also knew I was in the wrong and couldn't back down without him accepting responsibility for something. Ladies, you know what I mean, right?

Regardless of how irrelevant my theory was, let me share it with you. As you know, hubby was a virgin when we met, because of an overly tight foreskin which resulted in circumcision. What you don't know, is how difficult he found the circumcision. He can laugh about it now, mostly due to how much I laugh about it and I think he feels the need to join in. Just for fun, let me tell you in detail how my husband lost a part of his penis.

On the morning of the operation, Hubby's mum insisted on driving him to the hospital. He would have preferred to drive himself, but the doctor made it quite clear this was not an option. As my mother-in-law is an escaped mental patient (another one of my theories), and hubby was a young man who couldn't tolerate her nonsense, the day got off to a bad start. Having bickered most of the way to the hospital, he had to convince her not to enter the changing room with him when he was putting on his gown. She grudgingly sat in the waiting room, despite him telling her repeatedly to go home and he would phone when he was done.

As the nurse led him through to the cubicle, hubby asked if he was to shave himself first or would the doctor do it – his genitals he meant, not his face; he knew he wasn't in a Turkish barber. The nurse explained that they no longer shaved patients so the operation would be carried out with a full thatch, though she obviously didn't say thatch, as she was a medical professional.

This didn't sit well with hubby and his OCD, but he trusted they knew what they were doing. Gown on, he was wheeled into theatre and duly put to sleep. The op went without a hitch and he was wheeled into recovery, apparently screaming for his sister. I say 'apparently', as he can't remember this or indeed the recovery room. It was hubby's first experience of a general anaesthetic, which obviously did not agree with him.

Once he had regained full consciousness, they doped him up with painkillers to dull the ache between his legs. His swollen todger was heavily bandaged with just the tip of the head poking out, giving it the appearance of a bald Mummy.

Desperate to get home, he badgered the nurses to let him leave. Clearly, he was in no fit state, given his reaction to the anaesthetic, but in his thick head he was fine. Eventually, one of the nurses agreed that if he could pass urine he would be allowed to leave. This is the male equivalent of a woman going for her first poo after giving birth. Except, obviously that is real suffering, as women could literally shit out their womb. For a man this was just as terrifying.

After shuffling to the toilet, he closed the door, the nurse waiting on the other side. Positioning himself in front of the toilet, he pulled out his Tutankhamun, and steadied himself for the pain.

Having never been able to pull his foreskin back before, whenever he had gone for a wee pre-op, the urine would balloon at the end of his penis before gushing out. This was to be the first time it would flow unrestricted by a fleshy hood. (He has asked me to stop referring to his foreskin as a fleshy hood, but I never will.) This was to be confusing for the urine, which could not decide which way to go. And as he began to piss, it went in five different directions, none of them down the toilet. If a woman just had part of her penis removed, she would have applied some common sense and sat down to urinate, but as penises tend to be connected to men, they don't come with much common sense.

After a couple of attempts at redirecting the flow, he had to concede it was a losing battle, bearing in mind, though, that at this point he could still have sat down. Instead he opted to pee freely. He pissed all up the walls, over the floor and even across the mirror above the sink.

The effort of the whole affair was making him feel faint, but hubby has always been as considerate as he is stupid. There was no way he would ask anybody else to clean up his mess. Armed with handfuls of toilet paper he started to mop up his pee, and catching the sight of himself in the mirror he knew he wasn't well enough to go home. Not that that was going to stop him.

The nurse, becoming a little concerned about how long he was taking, was banging on the door. Composing himself, he took a deep breath and opened the door. 'Ta Daa,' he exclaimed with a big smile on his face.

The nurse, convinced by his ruse (or sick of his shit), agreed to let him go home after the doctor had spoken to him. The doctor duly sent him on his way with a bag of dressings, painkillers and the stern warning of, 'Don't get an erection for fourteen days or you will burst your stitches.'

If you are reading this and you are a man, or even if you are not a man but have met a man, then you will know that the likelihood of a twenty-one-year-old man not getting an erection for fourteen hours, let alone fourteen days is nil. Hubby went to bed that night and woke the next morning with wet pants. Inexplicably, he thought he had pissed the bed, although having not done that since he was four, I don't know why he jumped to that conclusion. As you have probably guessed, upon looking in his pants he discovered it was blood.

Like in an old-school horror film, his Mummy had risen from the dead during the night and come looking for blood. Or, if you prefer, he got a stiffy and burst one of the stitches on the underside of his penis.

To listen to him retell the tale there was several pints of blood and he nearly died. In reality there was some minor bleeding and the doctor opted not to re-stitch it. But the consequences of all this led to what hubby describes as the most embarrassing two weeks of his life. To cut a long story short, because they never shaved his balls and he now had an open wound, his penis ended up infected. This meant it had to be constantly bandaged and the dressings had to be changed every time he went to the toilet. He didn't like to be reminded of the fact that his penis was infected, which meant he didn't want to look at it, let alone re-dress his bandages, so he imposed a strict two toilet breaks a day policy. Once in the morning and once fourteen hours later.

To add to the suffering of the infection, the head of his penis was obviously very sensitive as this was the first time it had taken its fleshy hood down. He couldn't even put on underwear as it was too painful, which was a problem because he was recuperating at his mum and dad's house. With the best will in the world nobody wants to see their adult son's infected member flailing about over dinner, especially when everybody in the house knew that he burst his stitches getting a boner.

To save any embarrassment, he applied the same common sense that saw him soak a hospital toilet in piss and hatched a plan. His mum and dad came home from work to find their son, sitting in the living room, legs spread, wearing one of his mum's skirts. So, not only did they know their deviant son couldn't stop himself from getting an erection following an op on his cock, but he was also a crossdresser.

What he failed to consider when dipping his toe into the world of transvestism, was that he was due to get regular visits from the district nurse. He only remembered as she rang the doorbell, and to really ramp up the toe-curling humiliation of the situation, the nurse, Sarah, was an old school friend's mum. If she was surprised by hubby being done up like a young Mrs Doubtfire, she didn't show it and marched through to the living room.

Following a brief chat, she asked to see his wound. This left him with a dilemma, should he remove the skirt and be completely naked from the waist down? Or should he lift it up at the front, like a crossdressing flasher?

He went for crossdressing flasher and she got on her knees to inspect his willy. Like most houses, the living room of my in-laws' house is at the front of the property and looks out to the street. Hubby had suggested that they should perhaps close the curtains, but Sarah poo-pooed this and said she would only be a moment.

As he looked out the window, hubby could see his mum's elderly neighbour, Vivian, staring in, open mouthed, as he held his skirt up high. All he could do was wave sheepishly as she looked on, at what appeared to be her young neighbour getting a blow job from a mature nurse, whilst wearing his mother's skirt.

This wasn't even the bottom of the barrel for him in terms of embarrassment. As he sat alone one day, half of him dressed like a middle-aged woman, an event happened that rocked the world. Al Qaeda flew two planes into the World Trade Centre.

I am sure you will remember how huge this was, one of the few occasions in my lifetime where the news has interrupted scheduled programmes. Hubby was phoning my mother-in-law at her work to give them regular updates as they didn't have access to a TV, and this was before everybody had the internet. Just as the first building collapsed, the doorbell rang. It was Graham, the delivery driver for the local pharmacy, bringing hubby new dressings and painkillers. He was an older gentleman, who hubby knew to say hello to in passing, but this was the first time he had met him in a professional capacity.

He still doesn't know how to explain what he did next, but I think I get it because I remember watching the events unfold on the TV that day. There was a complete sense of disbelief, nothing this big had happened in our lifetime. I was with friends, though, and we were able to share our shock with each other.

Hubby was alone, and had been all day, as he had been every day for over a week. The calls to his mum only lasted a few seconds.

Throwing open the door, Graham barely had time to register the skirt before hubby took him by the hand and led him into the living room. It took a while as he was walking rather gingerly – hubby that is, not Graham.

As the world watched on in horror as the events unfolded that fateful day, my husband and his rancid penis, stood watching, with an old man, who he quickly realised was scared and possibly there against his will. He released his captive and went back to calling his mum.

There was briefly, one positive thing to come out of the whole affair, but cruelly it didn't last. After taking a bath, hubby had stood to get out of the tub when he caught his reflection in the mirror. The swelling caused by both the op and the infection had increased the size of his penis significantly. He mistakenly thought that removing the foreskin had allowed his penis to grow to its full potential. This is because he is a moron, and I mean that in a loving way.

He described it as being so large it didn't look human. Here's the kicker though, he also said it was angrily purple, unnaturally so. Clearly not a penis in its normal state. Anybody with half a brain would realise this was all connected to swelling from the operation and wouldn't last. Which it didn't.

I'm sure you would agree that hubby's experiences during his circumcision had no place in the argument, but I love to take any opportunity to bring up the time he dressed up like his mum.

My very own Norman Bates.

Chapter Twenty

Allie

Leave your hat on...

There are few prerequisites to having an intimate wax. Firstly, you must have hair, and that hair must be long enough to be waxed. Secondly, you can't be contraindicated, for example certain medications rule people out. Other than that, there really isn't anything else stopping you from having hair-free genitals.

Unless of course, you refuse to remove your knickers. You would be surprised how often people come in and are genuinely shocked that they must remove their underwear to have an intimate wax.

When they question me on why I am asking them to remove their pants, as though I am some sort of pervert, I always give them the same response, 'Well, you wouldn't keep your hat on at the hairdresser, would you?'

Amazingly this always seems to work. It immediately makes them realise that they are the one being unreasonable and that I am not a weirdo.

Not Allie, though. She has been coming to me for years now and still refuses to remove her knickers. Instead she moves them around a little at a time.

I don't know if you can imagine how frustrating that is but let me try to put it into context for you. Even if you don't work in an office, I'm sure at some point in your life you have used a computer. Imagine it is your job to use a computer, but when you turn up for work your boss has covered the screen of your monitor with post-it notes. As you work, she removes one post-it note at a time but replaces it before removing the next one. And the entire time she makes you feel dirty for wanting to look at the whole screen.

To make it as hard as possible, Allie wants me to wax the whole screen – I mean, whole vagina. Every time she wants a Hollywood wax, but she just won't take her pants off. I feel like Bill Oddie on Springwatch, trying to coax some woodland animal out of its lair.

It's even more bizarre because she has three children. So, either she has had to get her fanny out completely on at least three separate occasions, or her children had to force their way into the world past her knicker elastic.

Imagine the odds of that one sperm, fertilising the egg, travelling down the fallopian tube and attaching to the inside of the uterus. Once there it begins to form the embryo and placenta, then the brain and spinal cord begin to form and the tissue that will form the heart begins to beat. Buds for limbs appear, and eyes, ears, and nose begin to develop. Before eight weeks has passed all major organs and body systems have begun to develop. Buds for teeth appear and bones and muscles begin to grow. The intestines form and before you know it the kidneys are functioning and producing urine. Hair grows, the brain develops, the eyes begin to open, and lungs are fully-formed but not yet functioning. The foetus kicks and stretches, and during the last month of pregnancy gains about half a pound per week.

Then, after forty weeks, this miracle of life is ready to be born. During the first stages of labour, contractions make the cervix gradually open. As contractions become more regular, the waters break and as the cervix becomes fully dilated, the baby moves further down the birth canal towards the vagina, and after some pushing the baby's head is born.

Unless you are Allie's baby and you are met with a pair of Marks and Spencers cotton knickers, blocking your moment of glory, as your mother eyes the midwife suspiciously for wanting to look at her foof.

However, even for someone like myself, who has seen hundreds, if not thousands of fannies, the sight of one can still catch you by surprise. Apart from hubby, I have never told anyone this next story, and after I told him, he wished I hadn't.

One night after work I was running Christmas gifts along to my in-laws' house. As it was after 8pm I didn't want to ring the doorbell, as my father-in-law goes to bed ridiculously early. Instead I walked around the front to knock on the living room window.

Have you ever seen something so horrifying that it unnerves you, but you can't avert your gaze?

I have.

Sitting in the living room was my mother-in-law with her nightie pulled up over her waist, holding one leg in the air and plucking pubes out of her fanny with a pair of tweezers. Yes. In her living room. In front of the window. Why? She has two bathrooms.

I had a dilemma. She was expecting me to come along with the gifts and I didn't want to ring the bell, but if I knocked the window it would be beyond awkward. As I was debating what to do, she looked up and we made eye contact. I instinctively waved, and she waved back, the tweezers still in her hand and leg still in the air. The strangest thing about it was, neither one of us mentioned it when I went in. And neither of us have ever mentioned it since.

When I told hubby, he was horrified and pretended to gag. He didn't find it at all funny when I told him to calm down because his mum's fanny was just the front door to his first house.

I just feel for poor Vivian across the road. Between the crossdressing son flashing his swollen member, and the hirsute mother flashing her lady garden, the poor woman has seen too much.

Chapter Twenty-One

Steph

Too much info...

Although I incorrectly accused hubby of being prudish during the argument about Arthur's massive balls, he *does* suffer from selective prudishness.

Honestly, he is an absolute oddball. He can happily tell strangers at a party about the time he shat himself, but when he is around women, he categorically cannot talk about sex. Whether it is innuendo or straight-out sex chat, he clams up.

He puts this down to his awkward teenage years, when he couldn't talk to girls because he had put them on a pedestal. He thought they were some sort of heavenly beings, who he wasn't worthy of talking to. This became worse after he finally plucked up the courage to ask a girl out.

He was fourteen and Lesley was a year younger. He decided to phone her as he couldn't bring himself to do it face to face.

This was back in the good old days, when there was no mobile phones and the family phone was in the hallway of the house. Her mum answered the phone and he asked to speak to her daughter, and he could then hear her in the background telling Lesley there was a boy on the phone for her. When she came to the phone he introduced himself with his full name, because he has always been nothing if not formal, and asked if she would like to go out some time.

Her three-word reply stopped him from asking anyone else out for years. She said, 'No, it's okay.'

He said it was the 'it's okay,' that really stung. The 'no' he could have coped with, but the 'it's okay' felt like she was turning down a snack someone had offered her, something inconsequential – which is then how he viewed himself. A huge shame because he was a good kid and he gave up too quickly.

If this seems a little heavy, let me tell you the hilarious bit: not only was Lesley his best friend's cousin, but she was also his next-door neighbour. Who he walked to the school bus stop with every single day and had to do so for another five years after that phone call.

Any sane-minded individual would maybe have started with someone from the next estate, at least. But not my hapless Romeo.

As we ladies know, women are not heavenly beings. Anybody who has been in a ladies' public toilet can testify to that. I have been in toilet cubicles where there are footprints on the toilet seat. What crazy bastard is standing on the toilet for a pee? And as well as being hygienically challenged, many women are filthier than men sexually, I know because they tell me. (Even though I don't ask.) I have one client, Steph, who participates in sexual acts I previously thought were forms of assault, about which she insists on giving me a blow-by-blow description.

Hubby had only ever met Steph a couple of times before to say hello to, but I had told her all about him, as I do with most of my clients. He in turn knew nothing about her and had no idea about her predilection for risqué sex.

One day, when returning from the supermarket, hubby crossed paths with Steph as she was getting into her car, after her wax. This is the conversation that took place between them:

Steph: 'Hello.'

Hubby: 'Hi, there.' (I could immediately tell from his demeanour that he didn't remember who Steph was.)

S: 'I've just been in for a wax.' She nodded towards her fanny. 'I'm doing a marathon at the weekend.'

H: 'Oh amazing, good luck.' (From his expression he clearly thought she wasn't in any physical shape to be running a marathon. Which, to be fair, she wasn't.)

S: 'A sex marathon.' (She grinned like a lunatic.)

H: 'Um, okay, have you got a sponsorship form or something?'

To summarise, then, my middle-aged client tells my husband she is going to be having a sex marathon with her other half, for the whole weekend, and due to his awkwardness, he offers to sponsor them. I don't know how the payment structure would work for that: £1 per spank or £5 per orgasm? I don't think he thought that through. Either way, it's unlikely we'll be seeing Lenny Henry asking people to donate money to Comic Relief through sponsored orgies anytime soon.

Fortunately, Steph thought he was joking and drove away laughing.

Thankfully, I am not as prudish about sex as he is, which is just as well. You would be amazed how many women turn up for a wax, having just had sex. And by that, I mean they have brought the evidence along with them, so even if they don't tell me, I can see it for myself. At that point I politely tell them to bugger off and come back when they aren't leaking. Not because I am in anyway prudish, but because I don't get paid enough to clean jizz out of pubic hair.

My client Jane came in one morning quite distressed as she and her husband had had sex. Having both woken up before their son, they took a rare opportunity to have an early fumble. She was so apologetic, complaining it hadn't even been worth it, especially when she remembered she was booked in with me. In panic she had taken the head off her power shower, and inserted the hose into her vagina, giving herself a power douche.

Whilst I appreciated her effort to rinse out her fanny, I had to give her a ticking off. The vagina is like a self-cleaning oven: fine to stick meat in, and if you spill a little gravy you don't need to manually clean the inside of it. If anything, you can upset the Ph., and wash away healthy secretions. From the vagina that is, not the oven.

In recent years, educating my clients on what they shouldn't be doing with their vaginas has become a regular part of my job. It is not something I ever envisaged myself having to do when dealing with adults, but you would be amazed at what people do with their genitals.

A recent trend is the vaginal cucumber cleanse, which is far worse than it sounds. Women are peeling cucumbers and inserting them into their fannies, rotating them for up to twenty minutes, all under the misapprehension that it cleanses their vagina and neutralises Ph. This is not even pseudoscience, it is just outright lunacy.

The only way they are going to alter the Ph of the vagina, is by washing out all the good bacteria, which is what keeps the correct balance. Added to that, the cucumber could play host to any number of pathogens, including fungi, which you really don't want to introduce to your lady garden.

Personally, I think the whole cucumber cleanse stems from a husband coming home early from work. Leaving his keys at the door and hanging his jacket up, he went through to the kitchen and found his wife pleasuring herself with a cucumber. Too embarrassed to admit the truth, and thinking on the spot, she made up a load of nonsense about a vaginal cleanse. As a man, he had no frame of reference to doubt her, but to validate her lie she encouraged her girlfriends to do it. Which they did, and before long one of them filmed an instructional video on YouTube and it became a 'thing'.

I told hubby my theory, and he said, 'Just as well it was a cucumber, then, it would have been a much harder sell if she had been using a butternut squash.'

I have no idea why he said this, but if I'm being honest, I have stopped trying to understand how his mind works.

For those ladies who feel like a cucumber just isn't cutting it, they can also partake in vaginal steaming. This is the practice of sitting above a heat source on which water is placed. The belief is that the steam cleanses the vagina and uterus. Of course, this is absolute tosh and is of absolutely no benefit at all. The only way it would be of any use, is if you did it with a cucumber in your vagina, and you were looking to pickle it.

If you are thinking, well at least nobody is shoving rocks up their vagina, then I am afraid I must shatter your faith in evolution. Because, in our modern world, at the most technologically developed age in our existence, women are indeed shoving rocks up their vaginas. Jade eggs are semi-precious stones, which are carved into an egg shape, so that they can be popped into the vag. Supposedly, this awakens sexual prowess and helps maintain good health into old age. I am no scientist, but I am calling bullshit on this.

Nature is usually a good indicator of whether something is beneficial or not. In the Western Amazon basin, near the border with Peru, hundreds of macaws gather to eat clay. This is a natural source of salt in their sodium-poor diet and it helps remove toxins, such as tannins that they ingest from the plants they eat. Some species of fish can change sex in response to hormonal cycles or environmental changes. Amazing adaptations to ensure the survival of the species. But, to my knowledge, absolutely no animal species are shoving rocks up their fannies, as there is absolutely no point to it.

Human beings, so advanced that we have travelled to the moon and brought rock samples back, only for someone to think, 'I bet that would feel great in my vagina.'

I despair every time I need to dissuade clients from participating in any of these dubious practices, which is more often than you may think.

So, if you can't beat 'em, join 'em. Coming soon, I am launching my own range of cucumber-flavoured, jade stones with self-contained steam unit.

Chapter Twenty-Two

Gran

A leopard changes its spots...

I am very fortunate to be in as demand as I am, particularly given the state of the economy over the last few years. As I am self-employed, I have never quite been able to shrug off that fear of turning work away. Due to this, I am probably guilty of being too accommodating. I will book clients in for first thing in the morning, right through to last thing at night.

It is only at hubby's insistence that I take a Sunday off. Traditionally, in the beauty industry, salons are closed on a Monday – so that's when I treat all my beautician clients. People who work in beauty salons which offer waxing, choose to come to me on their day off, as I am so serious about the treatment.

Even doing something that you love can become too much if you don't step away from it occasionally, and it took a life changing event for me to fully realise this.

For as much as my childhood was bleak, there were two shining lights that made it bearable. My gran and grampa. Without them I wouldn't be who I am today. I loved them both equally, but I had a special bond with my grampa. He was everything that my father wasn't. Smart, funny, caring, hard-working, and an absolute gentleman.

We shared a love for physics and space, aeroplanes, and basically anything geeky. He instilled in me, my love for travel, which I have passed on to my children. And most importantly, he showed me that I didn't need to settle for the life it seemed I was destined to have. He was eighty when he died, after a short stay in hospital. I know eighty sounds old, but he never seemed it. He looked and acted like a much younger man.

Grampa was the first person I lost, who truly meant something to me. It floored the whole family, because Grampa was very much the lynchpin that held everyone together but I took it especially hard. If you have ever lost anyone that close to you, you know what I mean when I say a part of me died with him. Time softens the sharpness of the pain, but it never takes it away.

I stopped working completely for two weeks after he died, but one of the downsides of self-employment is, if you don't work, you don't get paid. It was difficult going back, particularly as my clients are so lovely, and they knew how close I was to my grampa. As they were all keen to check how I was, it meant having to rehash the story at least twice an hour, which never got any easier.

My mantra of, 'find the funny', had abandoned me for the first time in my life. For a while, I didn't think I would ever find anything funny again, I was consumed by grief. Unexpectedly, it was the change in my gran that forced me to laugh again. Mostly because, if I didn't I would have killed her. As I mentioned earlier, Grampa was the most prudish man you could ever meet, and I'd thought Gran was the most prudish woman – never a hair out of place, smartly dressed and well-spoken always. In my entire life, I had never heard either of them swear, even as an adult.

So, you can imagine my surprise, as I sat at my then seventy-five-year-old grandmother's table hearing her utter the words '...that old cunt, whoring about town.'

The 'old c' in question, was my grampa's eighty-nine-year-old sister. To be honest, she is a bit of a 'c', but at eighty-nine, she certainly wasn't whoring anywhere.

The absurdity of it made me laugh out loud. And thus, began my gran's descent into madness. Despite her age, Gran isn't the stereotypical old lady. We jokingly call her Dolph Lund-gran, due to her uncanny similarity to Hollywood actor,

Dolph Lundgren. That is, if you left Dolph out in the sun for forty years, shrunk him by two feet and prevented him from ever exercising. Gran has been on a diet since the 1960's, but her butt just gets bigger, year on year. Basically, they have the same haircut – circa his Ivan Drago from Rocky years, and not his current Expendables look.

Gran's friends are about twenty years younger than her, so she, like my grampa, has always appeared younger than her years. Losing her husband seemed to age her rapidly, and she went from a fun-loving, active, older woman to a cranky old lady. We had always assumed she was the driving force in their relationship, appearing to be the more motivated of the two, but with hindsight, it's clear Grampa kept the show on the road. Every decision he ever made was considered, he never jumped into anything impulsively. It was Grampa who dealt with all the household maintenance, did the driving, booked and organised the holidays, paid the bills, and so on.

In a nod to their generation, Gran did the cooking and cleaning. Granted, these are both very important elements in any relationship, especially my gran and grampa's. This was highlighted a few years previously when my gran went to Las Vegas for a week with her friends, leaving Grampa to fend for himself. I phoned him on the first night she was away to check how he was getting on. He reassured me he would be fine, as he had made four slices of toasted cheese, which would last him the week. What he didn't tell me, was that after dropping gran at the airport, he had gone to the supermarket on his way home, bought a loaf of bread, a block of cheese, and enough beer and Jack Daniels to stock a Student Union's Freshers' Ball.

He then proceeded to do what all men do when left to their own devices, reverted to his teenage self. I visited him on day four, to find him wearing his pyjamas and a robe, which he clearly had been wearing since day one. He was unshaved, very unlike him, and he was absolutely hammered.

At the time I was so annoyed with him, assuming without my gran he had fallen apart. I understand now he was just letting loose because he didn't get the opportunity to do it very often. Largely because he had to stay on top of my gran: for fifty-three years of marriage he had censored her outbursts and prevented her from ruining strangers' days.

I know this first hand, as I have since had to fill the role. Every time I take her shopping, I need to stand behind her, mouthing, 'I'm sorry', to the checkout operator as she unleashes a tirade of abuse about the 30p carrier bag charge. Every single time, she acts like the girl at the till has personally implemented the policy. Despite repeated attempts to explain that it is government legislation, she still blames Tracey from Tesco.

As the months went by, following Grampa's death, her outbursts became more frequent. Without him acting as a conduit for calm and reason she really lost it. My grampa was a very proud man, and he didn't believe in getting something for nothing. He believed you had to work for everything, to the point where he wouldn't use a coupon, even if it got him something for half price. I had always assumed my gran was the same. I was wrong.

She seems to think that if you live to a certain age, then you shouldn't have to pay for most things. Inexplicably, this includes but is not limited to: electricity, taxis, a new central heating system, windows and carrier bags.

As Gran's new persona began to develop in the weeks following Grampa's death it was like I was mourning the loss of both grandparents. It became clear that things would never be the same.

I was struggling, and with the first anniversary of his death looming, hubby had an idea. He knew it was going to be a particularly difficult time, so he suggested hiring a villa in Spain for the summer, to get away with Gran and the kids. The thinking being it would be just a little easier in different surroundings. His plan was to stay at home and work before joining us for a week over the anniversary.

Everyone agreed it was a good idea, and so without fully understanding what lay ahead, I organised everything.

Upon arriving in Spain, almost immediately I realised it was a mistake. My gran can speak Italian, she took a course at university along with my grampa, because their daughter relocated to Italy. She cannot however, speak Spanish. This did not deter her at all, insisting that, 'Modern Spanish is pretty much the same as modern Italian.'

Although my gran is old, I don't think she is technically old enough to refer to languages as modern. She was not around in the times of Ye Olde English, so I doubt she remembers old Italian or Spanish. Regardless, she spoke to every Spanish person she met with gusto, in Italian. The British are renowned across Europe for refusing to learn a second language, and keen to attract money from tourism, many Europeans speak English, particularly the Spanish. What they haven't learned is Italian, so many of the people my gran spoke to, told her in English that they didn't speak Italian. Even faced with a Spaniard who spoke her native tongue, she insisted on speaking to them in Italian, as if by osmosis they would suddenly pick up a language that they didn't speak. The Spanish are a proud people, and they did not take kindly to the suggestion that they are basically Italian.

I do speak a little Spanish, so I was able to explain that my gran was a little 'loco'. And had that been the extent of her holiday madness, I could have dealt with it.

What I wasn't expecting was the leopard print swimsuit she busted out upon arriving at the villa. It left little to the imagination, and my gran, usually quite self-conscious, turned into an exhibitionist.

Her insanity hit a new high when the kids and I returned from picking up hubby at the airport. He was joining us for the second week of the holiday, and I don't think he was prepared for the sight that greeted him upon his arrival at the villa.

My gran, adorned in her leopard print swimsuit, was sprawled across a sun lounger, her buttocks hanging over the side. Not a believer in sunscreen, she had basted herself in baby oil, and was glimmering in the morning sun. As a visual this was enough, particularly for hubby, but Gran wanted to make it weirder still. Feigning relief, she said, 'Thank god you're back. I was panicking for a bit there, lying here like this,' she gestured up and down the length of her body with her hand, 'and with them over there, anything could have happened.'

The 'them' she was referring to, were two young Spanish men cleaning the communal pool, at the rear of the property, and the 'anything', she was referring to was sex.

These men were barely twenty-one and physically in the prime of their lives. Every morning they came to tend the pool, and every morning my gran would offer them water, in Italian, dressed as the saddest big cat you have ever seen. And every morning, with fear in their eyes, they refused.

The pool boys got off lightly; Alejandro, the gardener wasn't so lucky. I received a call from the local property manager to advise me he was working the following morning. She explained he was paid directly by her, he didn't speak a word of English, and so just to let him get on with his work. I shouldn't even have mentioned this to Gran as nothing good could have come of it.

Sure enough, the scene next morning was like something from a David Attenborough documentary – if it had been directed by Wes Craven.

The kids were still sleeping, so I took the opportunity to sit on the upstairs balcony and take in the early morning sun. From my elevated position I could see her, adorned in her Lycra, spotted, battle costume. Like the proud leopard of the Serengeti she was stalking her prey. Unlike the leopard she couldn't scale the tree in the back garden to get a higher vantage point, so she had dragged a sun lounger behind it and perched on the edge of that. Coated in oil, Gran gleamed in the early sun, like a freshly polished car. IT wasn't ideal for hunting, but she hadn't reached her goal of dark mahogany yet.

Clutched in one hand she had an open, warm, two-litre bottle of Lemon Fanta, which the kids had opened the night before, drank half of, and left out on the patio. In the other was a crisp ten euro note. At this point I had no idea what was about to happen, but I certainly wasn't going to blow my cover and alert her to my presence.

Then Gran's head tilted, the big cat sensing her prey. Alejandro, a small man, probably in his mid-fifties, lean and wiry from years of manual labour, appeared wielding a leaf blower. I couldn't see his face at that point due to the straw hat he was wearing, which I regret as I would have loved to have seen his reaction.

A real leopard can reach speeds of up to thirty-six miles per hour and will try and get as close as possible to its prey before pouncing, typically within five metres. A gran leopard has a top speed of around three miles per hour and is physically incapable of pouncing at all. What she lacked in speed and physical prowess, however, was mitigated by the petrol-powered leaf blower drowning out her approach. The slap of her flip flops on the slabs was inaudible, even with the nerve damage in her left leg that caused her to throw it down like she was constantly trying to start the Haka.

Alejandro was distracted, looking at the ground as he tidied the borders of the garden with the blower. Then it was too late, she was on him.

The ensuing tussle was steeped in confusion and fear for Alejandro. Before he could get over the shock of being confronted by a dishevelled Bet Lynch, she was thrusting a half-empty bottle of warm Fanta and a ten euro note at him.

Confusing enough for the poor man, but even worse she was screaming at him in Italian.

Fight or flight kicked in and he fled, yelling in Spanish as he went. Younger and fitter than Gran, he should have made a speedy getaway, but Alejandro was encumbered by the blower and she nearly caught him.

It was at this point I intervened, fearing he might turn the blower on Gran to fend off her advances. Had he caught her under her not inconsiderable bingo wings he could have sent her on an upward trajectory, flying up into the clear blue sky never to be seen again.

After I led her back to her sun lounger, she explained sadly how she was just trying to give him a drink, as his must be hot work. When I asked about the ten euro note, she said it was a tip, 'as these poor people don't get paid enough, if anything at all.' In my gran's age-addled mind, self-employed Spanish gardeners are modern-day slaves, forced by their masters to carry out regular garden maintenance for holidaying Brits for little or no reward.

Alejandro was able to finish his work in peace, albeit constantly looking over his shoulder. I chose not to attempt to translate my gran's nonsense for fear of explaining it incorrectly and truly terrifying him. A couple of wrong words and he might think that my gran was trying to buy him for ten euros to work as a slave.

When I explained to hubby what had happened, he had his own theory on why Alejandro was so scared. He reckoned that as a regular worker on the resort he probably knew the pool boys, who had warned him about the horny pensioner at No. 5. Then next thing, she was advancing on him waving a tenner and an open drink.

'The poor man probably thought she was trying to pay him for sex and if that didn't work, she would get him to drink Fanta laced with Rohypnol.' How hubby laughed.

We didn't see Alejandro for the rest of the holiday. I can only assume he waited till we went out so he could work without being harassed.

It wasn't just the resort employees that Gran worked her magic on. She also managed to ruffle the feathers of the family in the villa next to ours. They owned the villa and it was a second home for them. They'd been holidaying there for over a decade, their kids learned to swim in the pool at the back of the properties. We hit it off with them immediately. Their son was significantly older than our two, but he was very good with them, making time to play every day. His younger sister was only a year older than our eldest, so they had more in common. Hubby, a self-professed hermit, even got on well with the dad of the family and everything was going swimmingly.

We all arranged to go out for dinner to the local bar and had a lovely evening: a nice meal and the drinks were flowing.

It all went so well that we invited them back to ours for a night cap. Sat round the table on the patio back at our villa the conversation was effortless. The sort of chat when you are getting to know new friends: work, kids, schools, holidays – you know, safe topics. Then Suzie, the mum of the family, mentioned that they had two cats. This prompted Gran to perk up, saying, 'I know a joke about that.'

Hubby knew immediately where this was going as he had spoken to her about it previously. He loves stand-up comedy, and when Gran mentioned, a few months ago, an English comedian she had seen on the TV, he knew exactly who she was talking about.

It was a certain part of this comedian's set that had struck a chord with my gran. This was due to her intense dislike of pets. She can't understand why anyone would keep animals in a house as she thinks they're unhygienic.

Knowing what was coming, hubby tried to stop her. 'No, you don't, Gran,' he said firmly.

'Yes, I do.' She was undeterred.

I too knew where this was going and tried to intervene, but she brushed me off. It only served to make our new friends more curious and they insisted that Gran tell the joke.

The first problem with gran's 'joke' was that it was not really a joke. It was an integral part of a set and delivered by a professional comedian in a way that was not at all offensive.

The 'bit' was split into three parts throughout the set and each part built up to a bigger laugh. The first part was the comedian asking the audience if anyone had a cat. People cheered and put their hands up to confirm that, yes, they did indeed own a cat. He then said, 'Your house stinks.' Sometime later he asked if there were any students in the audience. Again, people cheered and put their hands up. He then said, 'Your house stinks.' Later still he asked if there was anyone from 'up North' in the audience. And again, people cheered and raised their hands. He then said, 'Your house stinks.'

When he did it, it got a laugh each time. When Gran did it she was basically just repeating something she saw on the TV.

Effectively it went like this:

'Yeah, we have two cats at home,' said Suzie.

'Your house stinks,' said Gran.

Even if they had been friends of ours for years, it was still a brutal sentiment, delivered with the precision of a sledgehammer.

If you feel like perhaps Gran hadn't made the evening awkward enough, don't worry she wasn't finished. Suzie, obviously slightly miffed at the suggestion that her house wasn't clean, stressed she was very particular, and her home was immaculate, something that Steve, her husband, confirmed, explaining Suzie was obsessed with cleaning. As if she had to provide further proof that her home didn't stink, Suzie explained that her friends would have told her if there was a stench in her house.

Instead of taking this virtual stranger's word for it that her house was clean, Gran felt she really had to nail her point home.

'Well, I'm sorry Suzie, but if your friends have been in your house and you have two cats, and they haven't told you that your house stinks, then your friends are liars,' she said.

There really isn't much you can say to that. When a pissed-up, seventy-six-year-old, the colour of an Edwardian writing bureau, tells you that your house stinks and your friends are liars, it is better just to let it go.

Things haven't improved any since then, if anything she continues to get worse. She now lacks any ability to gauge what topics are appropriate for conversation in company. Just last week at my sister-in-law's birthday meal she decided to bring up the subject of my job. She announced at the table that she never understood the point of waxing the downstairs area, proudly adding that she had never in her life pulled, plucked, tweezed, shaved, or waxed a hair from her fanny.

I could see that hubby was already cringing and that was before his mother decided to pipe up. She added that it didn't really matter because as you get older everything just falls out and doesn't grow back. This resulted in hubby nearly bringing up his cannelloni.

My gran countered his mum by announcing that she was as hairy as ever around the old genital area, and

I don't think anyone at the table knew what to do with the information. My teenage daughter was particularly thrown, as was her friend who had joined us. Gran clearly picked up on this and addressed them about the importance of shaving their legs, because when they are getting amorous the last thing they want is friction burns.

Fortunately, when we were on holiday we hadn't noticed the state of Gran's foof, as nobody wants to see a leopard with spider legs.

CHAPTER TWENTY-THREE

Gail

IF YOU CAN'T STAND THE SMELL, GET OUT OF THE KITCHEN...

Life has a wonderful way of going full circle. This is how we end up with things like 'retro' clothing. Teenagers and twenty-somethings inadvertently ape the clothes of their parents' youth, while, ironically, classing said parents as too embarrassing to be seen with in public. Every generation thinks it's the first to see its elders as stuffy relics – fit for nothing other than the scrapheap. The young ones consider themselves the revolutionaries, the fire starters, the go-getters.

For those of us with a few decades under our belts, we've seen it all before. If this existence is a game, then Life will always be the winner, for no other reason than it has time on its hands. And we don't. The battle-hardened faces of the middle-aged commuters you see on the trains and buses every day, are testament to that. They too were once fresh-faced and ready to take on the world; to make their mark and right the wrongs. Then things get in the way: studies, work, bills, family commitments, health problems... the list goes on. You blink and there you are, a greying, middle-aged commuter hanging on to a handrail, in a too busy carriage.

Just as the globe circles the sun, our lives (if we are lucky enough, or unlucky, depending on your view) circle round too. You are born with someone cleaning you and wiping your shitty arse, and you die with someone cleaning you and wiping your shitty arse. The former, if you are fortunate enough, was probably your mum or dad dealing with your smelly effluence and the latter, an underpaid care worker with an understandable dislike of the elderly.

The bit in-between is your life, your story unfolding. Some are dealt a better hand than others and still mess it up, and some are dealt a dreadful hand and defy the odds to rise to the top. That top being whatever you choose it to be – wealth, success, fame, contentment, peace, love. We all have different ideas of what the perfect life is. Sadly, most people don't find their top, and to be fair, that's understandable because the odds are massively stacked against them.

Never in the history of mankind have we had so much yet felt so lacking. But lacking what?

Money – this is usually the first answer. If only I had more money I would be happy, we tell ourselves. Yet some of the unhappiest people I know are also the wealthiest. Conversely, some of the happiest people I know are financially the poorest.

Time – if I had more time, I would be happy. Not enough hours in the day, people bemoan. Usually you find the people who grumble about not having enough time are the ones doing the least. How does the old saying go, 'If you want something done, ask a busy man to do it' (or woman, as it is the 21st century, but then it is a very old saying).

Love – if only I could find my true love, I would be happy. Sorry, folks, true love is a Hollywood hoax and a very different beast from real love. True love that doe-eyed teenage girls dream of isn't real. Real love is hard-earned; fought for over months and years; accepting your partners flaws and mistakes, and they yours; making compromises in your life to benefit your other half and vice versa. Real love is messy and complicated, peppered with accusations and arguments, disappointment and betrayals. Along with a lot of acceptance, of the good and the bad to find the equilibrium – that's the *perfect* that people look for.

Stuff – this could be covered by more money, but there are so many people who just covet the latest... whatever. Car, mobile phone, T.V., clothes, and on and on. They are not satisfied now and sadly never will be.

Apologies if this has all got a little heavy, my aim after all is to try and make you laugh. I just wanted to illustrate to you why I try to find the funny when I can. It's because of that bit in between shitting yourself as a baby and as a geriatric – that bit, for the most of it, is yours. It's your story and you are the narrator. You might not be able to control a lot of things that happen to you or around you, but you certainly can control how you react. Me? I prefer to laugh.

Hubby is forever hitting out with a specific line whenever anybody complains to him about something, usually the kids. I don't know if he heard it somewhere, or if it drifted out of his strange imagination:

'We are all just hairless chimps on a dying planet.'

That's his way of saying, 'Does it really matter?' It may seem a little primitive (the saying not the chimps) but it's true. Ultimately, the little things in your life right now that are pissing you off, or making you sad – do they really matter? Will they still make you feel that way tomorrow, or next week, next month, next year?

I know that's not a cover-all sentiment. Some things do matter and massively so, but your response to them – could it be different?

When my grampa died, I didn't think I would ever laugh again. But I did, and I do. More now than ever, because this isn't your rehearsal, this is your life.

Anyway, all this imparting of wisdom is just my attempt at a clever way to lead up to telling you some more about people shitting themselves. Having read the first few chapters here, hubby pointed out that I may come across as a little puerile. He was less than impressed when I blew a raspberry at him. To be honest, I was less than impressed with the twenty minutes he spent pissing about with the page margins, or the virtual ruler, as he likes to call it.

Anyway, I presume you have now reassessed your life problems and are desperate for a laugh; you want to hear some stories about shitting.

If you are a parent, you will have countless tales of shit filled nappies. We all exchange tales of the 'worst one ever' at mother and toddler groups. Understanding looks and nods, exaggerated eye rolling, as each mum takes their turn to tell the group about 'shit so far up his back that it was in his hair,'

My personal stand out tale was often met with fewer understanding looks and more of horror. You see, generally in these kinds of circles it is accepted that you share some of the worse aspects of having kids, but in mixed company it is an unwritten rule that you don't go too far. I have always had problems seeing where the line is and usually by the time I have crossed it, it is a blur behind me, far behind me. I probably should have noted this the first time I told it, but I chose not too and continue to tell it to this day.

Now, out of respect for some level of anonymity, I won't divulge which one of my children is the protagonist here, as this could be a bit of a blot on their social standing. One morning I woke to the sound of this beautiful child singing in the next room. I leapt out of bed and grabbed my camera, so that I could film the beautiful scene for hubby to watch later.

As I rounded the corner of the hallway to the nursery, light bounced in through the window illuminating the Winnie the Pooh and friends adorning the wallpaper. I stood at the door for a moment, listening to the garbled, nonsensical words that my child pieced together to form a melody of sorts.

I couldn't wait any longer. Swept away in a wave of love I had to peek round the door for a look, my heart ready to burst. It took a moment for the full scene to sink in. Instead of the beautiful, blonde-haired, light of my life standing in front of me in the cot, dancing to the song they had created, there was a little, dark-haired child with their back to me; swaying along to the beat, whilst rubbing the wall with their right hand.

I rubbed my eyes, sure that they must be blurry from sleep. Nope, not blonde. The floorboards creaked underfoot, and this impostor turned to face me. And the full horror hit me.

My child had done a massive morning dump in their nappy and rather than alert me, chose to reach inside the elasticated hem, with both hands, and pull out fistfuls of shit.

It was smeared up and down every spindle of the cot, all over the bed linen, the Babygro – even darkening the once blonde hair. The hand that was rubbing along the wall caked Winnie, Piglet and Tigger in faeces. Eeyore looked on, his glum expression somewhat matching my own.

Worse than all of that, though, worse than any of the shit-fest that was taking place in front of me, was when I saw the left hand.

It was like the final scene in the thriller Seven, with Brad Pitt and Morgan Freeman. We all know what's in the box and we shouldn't look. But you know you need to. My child was shovelling their own shit into their mouth. Worst of all, they were smiling whilst they chewed it like a fillet steak in a nice restaurant.

That's the thing about mums in a posh town, they don't really want to hear about anyone eating their own shit. Even if it is a toddler. I made sure to tell all of them, though, because it made me laugh. And it still does; many years have passed since then and I am still laughing even as I write this. It was worth the two-hour clean up that came after the hour spent washing the young offender down, and brushing the crap out of their teeth.

The other benefit of this story, is that any time said child tries to get cocky with us we just say, 'Yeah, remember that time you ate your own shit? Shall we put the home video on?' Game over.

Now let me take you to the other extreme of the circle, to my ninety-two-year-old aunt. She defied all medical odds, eking out twenty years more than the doctors gave her. She battled bowel cancer in her early seventies, beating it and refusing to follow the subsequent dietary recommendations of her medical team, or indeed any of the lifestyle improvements suggested. Whilst this didn't seem to shorten her life, it did make it a little messier – for her nearest and dearest anyway.

Aunt Isabelle was a big dessert fan, particularly crème brûlée and panna cotta. Her bowels weren't so keen. The sweet, creamy desserts ran through her quicker than Usain Bolt on a crate of Red Bull. For the first few years, post-cancer, she managed to compose herself until she could reach the sanctuary of the closest toilet. Then, as time passed and her body slowed, she didn't always make it in time. Most of the family have a story about Aunt Isa soiling herself at a family event – having had two, three, sometimes four, desserts.

For most people that would have heralded a change in lifestyle, a self-imposed ban on sugary treats. Not Isa, she chose a different path and began buying adult nappies. A safety net for when she couldn't safely reach the porcelain throne.

This was met with varied reactions from family members. Some relatives were indifferent, they didn't see it as their problem, and others were furious. They couldn't understand why she wouldn't just eat better and stop shitting herself. Isa didn't care either way.

Initially, I thought it was nobody's business but hers, if after nine decades on this planet you can't have a pudding then what's the point? My view did change in the last couple of years of her life, though, because in all honesty it did seem like she had just given up on even trying to go to the toilet. She was still mobile at this point, enjoying day trips and slowly wandering around the shops. But the nappies seemed to be less safety net now and more porta-loo.

Standing at a sliver over five-feet, she certainly wasn't a tall woman, but was almost as wide as she was tall; she was big. And the real problem came when she was no longer flexible enough to clean herself after an incident. It then fell on whoever was closest, whether it was the home help or a relative, and towards the end, the staff of the nursing home.

My first experience of an adult nappy change was certainly an experience. By that point I had changed hundreds, if not thousands of nappies, but they all belonged to people that I could pick up with one hand.

It was after dinner at my Gran's house one Sunday that my relationship with my old auntie changed. We had all enjoyed a Sunday roast, with all the trimmings, and following the main we watched knowingly as Aunt Isa tucked into her panna cotta with gusto.

As we settled onto the sofa, leaving hubby and Grampa to do the dishes, we heard a sound akin to a hippo burping under water, erupting from the corner of the room where Isa had thrown herself onto the couch.

Her face expressionless, she seemed oblivious to the war cry from her bottom. Without her hearing aids in there was no chance she could have heard it, but even a good minute after the event her buttocks should still have been reverberating.

If the sound was bad, then the smell was unimaginable. It became clear almost instantly that this wasn't just gas, this was an adult sized nappy full of Gran's Sunday roast that Aunt Isa had turned it into her own brand of gravy. Still, no expression on her wizened face. Gran and I were the first to realise what had happened, the kids registered the smell but were yet unaware of the source.

Gran and I locked eyes, no words were spoken but a volley of facial expressions were exchanged. A silent battle of wills ensued to decide who would clean and change the matriarch of the family. A once proud, strong woman, now sitting in her own shit, gurning like she was chewing a wasp. If you find me a little harsh, and are feeling sorry for Aunt Isa, then please don't, as she was literally as happy as the proverbial pig in shit.

As well as being profoundly deaf, toothless, legally blind, and incontinent, she also suffered from dementia. Not that she was aware of this, which was a blessing, and any time you asked her how she was, you got the same answer, 'I am a lucky, lucky old woman. Just look at the family I have around me.' And that was true, for despite not having children of her own, she was never short of visitors.

Back to the matter in hand, I was yet to take a turn of changing Isa, as usually that fell to Gran as she saw her most often. The main problem was that at my gran's house there was no downstairs bathroom, and in her condition, Isa tended to avoid stairs.

After assessing the situation, I decided the only option was for me to act as an improvised, human stairlift. Positioning Isa at the bottom of the stairs, she held on to the handrail and I placed my shoulder at her derriere. I am fortunate enough never to have been involved in a war situation, but I imagine that the smell that emanated from Aunt Isa's rear end could easily be classed as a military grade chemical weapon. And as I pushed her up each stair, my shoulder pushed more noxious gas up my nostrils, which were only centimetres from ground zero.

The aroma was almost matched by the assault on my ears, as with each burst of movement they were filled with squelching noises not, I imagine, dissimilar to a lorry driving over a badger.

Having reached the safety of the top landing, I made a mental note to check out euthanasia clinics. Not for Isa, but for me, as the whole episode was leaving a stain on me mentally that I didn't think I could erase. Incidentally, Aunt Isa had left an actual stain on my jumper, which I probably could have erased with some Vanish, but I opted to just bin it.

Once in the privacy of the bathroom, I helped Isa undress, and her nappy fell to the floor with a thud. The weight of it caught me off guard and it slipped out of my grasp. When it hit the ground, liquid shit splattered everywhere, wetting the bottom of my bare legs.

I silently gagged, safe in the knowledge that she couldn't see my face clearly enough to discern emotion. Having quickly wiped my legs clean, I stripped down to my underwear to avoid any more 'staining'.

Fortunately, my grampa had installed a double shower, which allowed us both to fit in comfortably. My aunt's flat had a wet room installed long before for this very reason, as she could no longer manage to clamber into the bath. Without any instruction Isa automatically stood with her back to me, legs spread, arms over her head with hands placed flat against the wall. Just like a prisoner who was about to be patted down by a guard. It dawned on me it was what the home-helps got her to do when she soiled herself at home.

Isa stood patiently until I washed her, and then whilst I dried her, and then as I dressed her in my gran's clothes, as hers were ruined.

After that I wasn't so keen on Aunt Isa having desserts. In fact, whenever she reached for a crème brûlée, I, with the rest of the women in the room, ran for cover like someone was about to pull the pin on a grenade. Except instead of being full of explosives, it was full of shit. The men, safe in the knowledge that they would never be asked to shower Isa, would sit and chuckle to themselves and wait for the bang.

You may be wondering what any of this has to do with my job as a waxer. Well, brace yourself, for these were simply palate cleansers for what I can only say is the most disgusting story I have ever been told by a client. A story so vile that it made hubby retch and spit out his dinner – and that is saying something, because up until then hubby had never spat out food – even when he mistakenly ate a coal off the barbecue, thinking it was a well-done sausage. Too embarrassed to admit his mistake he ate it.

The story starts relatively normally, for me anyway, with my client Gail, talking about anal sex. Gail was in for her first appointment since returning from an amazing holiday in the Caribbean, but instead of being refreshed and relaxed, she had come back annoyed and frustrated.

Her frustration lay in the fact that, for reasons that she couldn't explain, she'd allowed her husband to stick it up her bum on holiday. Whether it was the natural beauty of the setting, perhaps the numerous cocktails, or maybe just out of mischief, she had got carried away and he bummed her.

Apart from the pain she endured, both during and after the experience, she was annoyed because she decided it would be sexy to suck his cock immediately after it. As you can imagine, that was not a particularly good idea, but she had seen it in a porno and thought it looked hot.

What Gail hadn't seen in the porno was that female porn stars go to great lengths to ensure they are clean. This includes having a douche immediately before filming, which cleans out the asshole.

Gail hadn't had a douche. Truth be told, Gail hadn't even showered since that morning and they had been at the beach drinking and eating all day.

Caught up in the moment she didn't even look at his penis as she wrapped her lips around it. If she had, she would have seen it was covered in shit. Her shit. And she swallowed some of it before she realised. But don't worry, it didn't stay down too long because she vomited all over his groin and the bed.

The Egyptian cotton sheets were splattered with regurgitated Cosmos, king prawns and faeces. In a competition of who was the most disgusted, Gail or her husband, it sounded very much like a draw.

If you think that is bad, then buckle up, because that is not the story that made hubby retch.

When Gail returned to the estate agents where she works, she told one of her colleagues about the experience. In a sense of, I'm assuming, misplaced comradery her colleague, Victoria, decided to share her own experience.

Victoria's tale started in a similar vein to Gail's. She and her husband Thomas had decided to try anal sex to spice up their lovemaking. And just like Gail, this resulted in a shit-covered member. In Victoria's case some shit had dropped from Thomas's todger on to her chest. Unlike Gail, though, Victoria found this aroused her, as did Thomas, and he rubbed the shit into her breasts. They finished making love with shite smeared all over her torso.

I won't lie to you, if hubby were to drop shit anywhere on my body, my own or otherwise, I think I would knock him out cold. But something had been awakened in Victoria and Thomas and they discovered a love of faeces, and they indulged this love in the most unimaginable way.

In probably the worst overshare I have ever heard, Victoria described to Gail, in detail, what her and her husband do for kicks.

Once a month when the kids go to stay at their grandparents, Victoria and Thomas cut open bin bags and tape them to the kitchen floor, cupboards and walls. Then having not been to the toilet since the night before, they shit all over each other and themselves. Massaging steaming hot shit into each other, they roll around in it whilst shagging.

When Victoria told Gail about her stinky, kinky fetish, Gail's face must have shown what she really thought about it, because a look of panic swept across Victoria's face and she feebly added, 'Please don't tell anybody.' Right. If somebody told me, unprompted, that they liked to shit all over themselves and their partner then roll around in it like pigs, I would tell everybody. And in their *kitchen* of all places – where you make your kids dinner. Dirty buggers. Literally.

Not that I had any reason to doubt Gail, but even for my line of work I found this story hard to believe. However, a quick search online taught me that coprophilia, also known as scatophilia, or scat, is the name given to sexual arousal from faeces. Worryingly, not only does this have a name, but limited studies on the topic show a frightening number of people indulge in it.

On a lighter note, if you do happen to take a dump on your partner's chest, you would be giving them what is known as a 'Cleveland Steamer', but for goodness sake please get their permission first.

Chapter Twenty-Four

Joanne

Who framed Roger Rabbit...

I have had various jobs over the years, some I liked more than others. My first job at thirteen was working at a fruit and veg stall. I say stall, it was technically an extremely narrow shop, nestled between Marks and Spencer and a fish and chip shop.

Although it was hard work, I loved that job as it suited my personality. Even at thirteen I had a big gob and liked the banter with the customers. I wasn't so keen on lugging sacks of spuds up and down the stairs, though, as the only storage space was above the unit.

It helped that I had a good boss, Tom the owner, who ran a few fruit and veg shops dotted about the county. Initially he was shocked that I was only thirteen, my height belying my age. He was reluctant to take me on, but I proved myself during a trial weekend and it wasn't long before I was opening and running the stall for him.

Tom had the misfortune of meeting my dad on a few occasions and quickly got his number. He was one of the few grown-ups that I opened up to about my home life, and I had to plead with him not to go around and batter my dad. That would only have made things at home worse. Instead, what he did was slip me extra cash because he knew my dad was keeping a check on my hours and deducting a share for himself.

What Tom didn't know at the time, and at first neither did I, was that my mum was also stealing money from the wages I was saving up in a tin at home. That probably upset me more than my dad demanding his share; I would have gladly given it to her if she asked.

As I got older I was able to boost my earnings by working nights in the local pubs. It never felt like work behind the bar, the buzz of it made it feel more like a night out. Unlike the quiet drinking establishments in hubby's hometown, all the pubs in my town had doormen. Strangely, when you grow up somewhere like that it doesn't seem that scary, violence was just something you expected. The only thing I worried about when a fight kicked off on a night out, was my drink getting spilled.

There was one shift, though, when I was working in one of the rougher pubs in town, that will always stick with me. It was a Saturday night and that day there had been a local derby game, the outcome of which decided the league winners. The rivalry between the two teams is legendary on a national level and it was not unheard of for fans on both sides to be murdered on game day.

The management had been expecting bother, so doubled the number of security staff and banned all football colours, not just the local teams.

The night had been going well and the door team had done a good job at weeding out potential troublemakers. Unfortunately, sometimes no matter how good a job you do, you can't plan for everything. A fight kicked off between two regulars, both rival fans which the door staff had been aware of. However, they assumed it wouldn't be an issue as they had arrived together and were, in fact, brothers.

What started as banter escalated into arguing, then shoving, and then fists. In a rage one of the brothers picked up a pint glass and shoved it into the other one's neck, right in front of me.

I could see the look of anger in his eyes dissipate, immediately replaced with a mix of fear and concern. He froze, the glass dropping to the floor. I also froze, my mouth open in disbelief, as with blood spurting from his neck he turned and covered me in it. Not only did it go all over my face but into my mouth and eyes .

Spitting on the floor, I rubbed the sleeve of my shirt on my face to clear away the worst of it. My manager threw me a cloth and told me to put it on the guy's wound, while he phoned for an ambulance and the police – clearly, he had seen it all before.

Looking down at the cloth I could see it was a dirty bar cloth that he had grabbed.

'This is manky,' I said, holding the cloth up.

'I think that's the least of his fucking worries, his heads nearly hanging off,' the manager yelled back.

This was not what the victim needed to hear, his eyes looking to me for reassurance that I wasn't able to give. Holding the filthy rag up to his wound was about as effective as any diet that my gran had ever been on. Blood seeped through the material and down my arm.

The police arrived first as they were always milling about near the pubs at the weekend. Rather than relieve me of my first aid duties, they concentrated on corralling the revellers, or as they called them, potential witnesses.

To be honest, they didn't have to do much corralling as barely anyone attempted to leave, since they hadn't finished their drinks. Only those in the splash zone had moved, and even then, just further round the bar. As for witnesses they would have had more luck finding Lord Lucan; this was not the kind of establishment where people would tell tales – including the man whose head was hanging off.

Fortunately, the paramedics weren't far behind the police and I handed the patient over to them. Miraculously, he survived and although (unsurprisingly) nobody saw anything, they were still able to convict the brother using CCTV footage from the bar.

Following the bar work, I got a job waitressing for a well-known chain restaurant, who, believe it or not actually trained their staff in silver service – despite never using it as they primarily sold fish and chips. It's barely worth mentioning, though, as then I moved onto my first grown up job, which was working at the Inland Revenue.

When you work for a Civil Service department you need to sign the Official Secrets Act, which sounds cool and mysterious, but it just means you can't divulge anything about your work. Which is just as well because nobody wants to hear it. As far as I am aware, though, it is okay for me to divulge that there are a lot of tossers working at the Inland Revenue, now known as His Majesty's Revenue and Customs. HMRC for short, but I'm sure you can think of many other four-letter words for them. To be fair, there were plenty of decent people there too. I would say it was roughly a 4:1 ratio of decent people to tossers.

I saw it as a job and nothing else, but there were employees there who were passionate about chasing people for taxes. It made me wonder what they were passionate about in their private life, kicking kittens?

So, I'm not allowed to tell you much about my time at the Revenue, which is just as well because I have blocked most of it from my memory. I can tell you that one good thing came from it, which is that I met hubby there.

I was aware of him before we first met because I thought his team was bullying him.

There was a relatively new celebrity chef on the scene at the time, one who had got his first TV programme a few years before: The Naked Chef, on BBC2. I had never watched the show, but it had been on in the background when I was round at a friend's house. Not paying full attention, I remember thinking how progressive it was that the BBC had given a cooking show to someone with learning difficulties.

That chef was a young Jamie Oliver, who it turned out didn't have learning difficulties, just a very large tongue that impeded his speech. Not knowing that, and not knowing that hubby had been making lunch for his team resulted in me having egg on my face.

As the office we worked in was so large, each member of staff had their name on top of their computer screen. Somebody in hubby's team had removed his name and replaced it with Jamie Oliver, in a nod to his cooking skills. I assumed that he too had learning difficulties and that the team were making fun of him.

Upon returning to my own team, I commented to my colleagues that the bastards in Team D were picking on the new start, which was terrible as he had learning difficulties. I failed to explain to them my skewed logic behind assuming that he actually did have learning difficulties, so word got out and a lot of animosity built up around the office towards the members of Team D.

It was only when I got talking to him on a works night out that I realised he didn't have learning difficulties, and when I told him about the mix-up he explained to me that Jamie Oliver didn't have learning difficulties either.

As well as seeing the funny side, hubby-to-be was quite relieved, as he had been wondering why people in the office had been speaking to him so slowly and nodding their heads a lot.

If you think that we had a laugh about it, and then he asked me out and the rest is history, then I am afraid you are wrong. He took the less direct route of asking my friend out first, because she happened to work in his team. At the time he didn't know she was notorious for playing mind games with guys, so when she said no he left it at that.

Her plan had been to toy with him for a bit and make him ask again before accepting. As much as he can be a boring bugger, he has never been a game player, so when she tried to string him along he just shut it down. He was hurt, though, as he had thought that they got along well. I took it upon myself to console him at the staff night out the following Friday. It turned out to be a great session; drunk hubby is way more fun than sober hubby, and he won me over with his surprisingly camp dance moves. Then, taking a break from dancing he turned to me and announced drunkenly:

'Do you know who would love you? My mum. How do you fancy going out with me next week and you can come and meet her?'

Unfortunately, he had chosen to ask me in front of all our colleagues from the office. Those who knew me well, sat open-mouthed, awaiting my response. They were aware I was not the dating type, having vowed never to get into a relationship again after my last one ended badly the year before.

There was something about him, though, that thing that you can't quite put your finger on. He wasn't the best-looking guy that had ever asked me out, nor the richest or the smartest, but he was the *right* one. If you think this a little harsh, he has agreed with all the above, but he is insistent I point out him out as the funniest person I have ever met.

Maybe that's it? Maybe I found my funny in him. Whatever it was, he's bloody lucky because if it had been anybody else it wouldn't have gone past the first date.

True to his word, he picked me up and drove me forty minutes to his parent's house, to meet his mum. I mean it in the nicest possible way, when I say that the woman is bat-shit crazy. Within sixty seconds of my meeting her she said, 'Wait to you see my new jacket.'

Disappearing into the hallway, she came back with what looked like a tablecloth from a tacky, 1980's Chinese restaurant and proceeded to try and make me wear it. If you have ever been in TK Maxx and seen an item of clothing and thought, 'Who would wear that?' the answer is my mother-in-law.

He then took me to a local restaurant which had been allowed to fall into disrepair, as the owners were preparing to tear it down and rebuild it. It was less rustic and more rubbish. During the meal I excused myself and went to the loo, where I phoned my best friend Maz. I had arranged for her to call me with an 'emergency' at an agreed time, so that I had an excuse to leave if the date was going badly.

I was just as shocked as her when I found myself telling her that I thought I loved him. This unnerved me, as I am not that type of girl. My experience with my dad made me a lot colder than most when it came to relationships with guys. But there was just something about hubby-to-be.

Following the meal, he took me to the cinema but having failed to check the listings, the only thing showing was Daddy Day Care, a children's film starring Eddie Murphy. There was a pub next to the cinema, so I assumed we would just go in there for a drink instead. Nope, we went and watched Daddy Bloody Day Care, with a cinema full of screaming children.

It was the best worst date I have ever had, and I knew then that I would spend the rest of my life with him.

I will always be grateful for my time at the Revenue, for the friends that I made, but most importantly for meeting my 'one'. But I am glad that I left when I did, as I don't think that I could have spent forty years behind a desk. The monotony would have killed me. Okay, I may not have had to deal with shitty arses and leaky willies, but I wouldn't be having as much fun as I do now.

Some might say my current job is monotonous, the same action performed repeatedly, thousands of times a week. Yet, it is my clients that make it anything but. Their lives and stories that have filled this book make me excited to go to work every day.

Clients like Joanne, whose job is way more exciting than any I have ever done. Although a regular, I only see her every few months as opposed to every few weeks, which is the norm. That is because she works and lives in London, having relocated to expand her business. Nestled in a basement apartment in a very exclusive area of the city, Joanne runs her business from her home.

I have only seen photos of her dressed for work, as when I see her, she is wearing jogging bottoms and a t-shirt ready for her wax. Her working clothes consist of various outfits made from either leather or latex, and killer heels, often adorned with spikes.

You may have guessed that Joanne works as a dominatrix. If you know what that entails – then good for you, you dirty bugger. If you are a little more innocent, which I doubt if you have made it this far, then let me explain.

Basically, wealthy men pay Joanne to inflict pain and humiliation on them in any way she sees fit. This includes, but is not limited to: slapping, spitting, kicking their genitals, and shoving butt plugs up their arses. Boundaries are usually drawn up in advance between the dominatrix and her client, and certain clients will request sessions that are a little more bespoke than normal. One client, let's call him Roger, has some very specific requirements when it comes to his session. Roger likes to dress up as a rabbit. Aww that's cute, you might be thinking, but Roger's rabbit suit is crotchless and what he gets Joanne to do may put you off root vegetables for life.

Joanne inserts a carrot into Roger's anus, the stalk still attached so that the leaves dangle from his arse. Then she straps him to a St Andrew's cross bondage frame and kicks him in the dick. For an hour. I flicked hubby in the balls once for a laugh and he *whined* about it for an hour.

Bearing in mind that Joanne's clientele includes businessmen and politicians (past and present), there is a strong chance that this man makes decisions that affect your daily life. We can only hope that if he is a politician he isn't claiming her hourly rate on expenses, as that is a scandal neither of the big parties could withstand in the current climate.

The thing which bothers me about that story is the carrot, and I have always meant to ask Joanne about it. Does she supply the carrot, or does he bring it with him? If he brings the carrot, is he just bringing one? Or is he bringing the whole bunch? Because if I worked in a shop and a man in a suit came up to my till, with one solitary, organic carrot, stalk still attached, I would assume that the carrot was going up his bum.

Equally, if he brings the whole bunch does he take the rest home with him or leave them at Joanne's? I don't know about her, but there is no way I could use any of the remaining carrots even though they never went near his rectum. And if he brings them home is his wife not wondering why the only thing he has bought at the shop is a bunch of carrots?

Finally, do you think Roger has excellent vision? Or does that only work if the carrot goes in the other end?

Whatever the fate of the carrots, whenever hubby puts Question Time on the telly, I can't help but try and work out which one of the politicians looks most like a rabbit.

Chapter Twenty-Five

Gregg

Denial not just a river in Egypt

As I touched on earlier, I have never been a girly-girl, either in personality or style. Sure, I like to get dolled up and go out with the girls, but I'm just as likely to be drinking pints of Guinness as I am cocktails.

My height has always been an issue when it comes to buying clothes, and more so in my youth. Most high street chains carry a tall range now, but it was a completely different story fifteen to twenty years ago and I have, on occasion, bought clothes from websites dedicated to crossdressers – styled with ladies in mind but made with dimensions for men. Fortunately, I'm more likely to be found in ripped denims and a faded band t-shirt, rocking out at a heavy-metal gig, than I am in hot-pants and a boob tube at a Katy Perry concert.

As a huge fan of live music, I tried to get hubby into metal. In the early days when we were just dating, I bought us tickets to a gig with a more mainstream line-up, just to test the water. I was buzzing; we were about to see Queens of the Stone Age, The Foo Fighters, Electric Six and the Red Hot Chilli Peppers. At the venue, hubby wasn't overly impressed, he immediately spotted the bank of porta-loos and the throng of people trying to get into them. I could see him mentally calculating how many hours he would need to go without using the toilet, and how many drinks he could have in that time. As an OCD sufferer, he would rather piss his pants than use a porta-loo.

When he discovered the cola was warm and the burgers were cold, I could tell he was incensed but was trying to keep a lid on it because I had bought his ticket.

The final straw then came when we took our places in the crowd to watch the bands. Something suddenly hit the back of his head, and putting his hand up to rub it, his hair was soaking wet.

'Someone has just thrown their drink at the back of my head. Why would they do that?' he asked confused.

'Erm, that wasn't their drink,' I answered cringing.

When I told him that it was more likely to be piss in the plastic cup that had smacked his bonce, he lost his mind.

'You dirty bastards,' he screamed repeatedly to the crowd behind him.

It took me quite a while to calm him down, his usual subdued demeanour replaced by a furious, piss-soaked Hulk. He spent the rest of the gig scanning the crowd for people throwing cups of piss. It was a long time 'til I could get him to go to another gig. I finally convinced him to go to Metallica, where he stood right at the back and complained that the lyrics were unintelligible. So, if you are reading this, James Hetfield, then hubby would like you to enunciate your words – if you don't mind – but please don't feel bad, James, as we are talking about a man, who, when we first met, had an entire music collection consisting of one CD called We Got Da Funk.

As well as his limited music collection, hubby's wardrobe left a lot to be desired. His favourite item of clothing, when we met, was a zip-up cardigan, which he insisted was sports-casual; the sport, I am assuming, being crown green bowls. It's not as if he had the same problem with choice as I did. Despite being a big guy he wasn't so gargantuan that he had to shop on specialist websites. Regardless of advances in high street fashion for bigger girls, even now it can be frustrating trying to find the right outfit for a big event.

Before I became a waxer I never considered this from the point of view of a crossdressing or transgender man, because in all honesty I had never met one. Now I know several. The first transgender client I treated was a man transitioning into a woman. Right up until I removed the towel I had no idea;

having booked using her female name and turning up as a very glamorous, well-dressed woman, there was nothing to suggest what was nestling beneath.

I won't lie, it was a bit of a shock – expecting a vagina and being confronted with a penis. Not Stephen Rea in The Crying Game kind of shock, but it did catch me off guard.

As the client, Dil, didn't address the elephant in the room, I just got on with waxing her, putting aside the fact that there is something a little surreal about waxing someone's balls when they have bigger tits than you do. The only problem I did have, was that I'd quoted Dil the price of a Hollywood for a woman, which is considerably cheaper than the equivalent treatment on a man. Before any gentlemen shout sexism, there is a lot more involved in waxing your balls. Some men have enough skin on their balls, that when stretched taught it could cover a tennis court. There's an image for you – some bloke's scrotum being used to cover centre court at Wimbledon during a downpour, as Sir Cliff Richard entertains the crowd with an impromptu performance of Summer Holiday. New balls, please!

Anyway, Dil wasn't best pleased when I charged her the full amount, but she did laugh when I said, 'I know, I'm a real ballbuster, right?'

That could have gone either way, but I think if there's a chance of a laugh you need to take a punt.

I have quite a few crossdressers and transgender people on my client list now, and to be blunt, some are more convincing than others, running the full gamut from Courtney Act to Mrs Doubtfire and everything in-between. I don't mean that in a mocking way, because the same could be said of all the women I've known my whole life – I have days when I could easily pass as a truck driver called Shug – but what I would say, is that if you're a man venturing out dressed as a woman, then *don't* borrow your nan's clothes.

Some of my clients dress-up part-time for fun, for others it's a full-time lifestyle choice. They all, however, are honest about what they do and why they do it. Apart from one.

The first time I spoke to Gregg was on the phone, when he was booking in for a full body wax. That means everything off apart from eyebrows, eyelashes and the hair on the head. Mid-way through the call Gregg, rather emphatically, said, 'I mean, I'm not gay.' This was completely unprompted, and I don't know about you, but if someone tells me unprompted that they aren't something, I automatically assume that they are. How many times have you heard someone say, 'I'm not racist but...' Stop right there, because clearly the next words out of your mouth are going to be extremely racist. 'I'm not a homophobe but...' Er, you just hate gay people? The only exception to that rule is when someone says, 'I'm not being funny but...' As invariably they are right, in no way are they being funny.

So, what did Gregg expect me to say? 'That's nice, congratulations on your heterosexuality.'

It was certainly a first for me, nobody had ever felt the need to confirm their sexuality when booking in for a wax before.

Fast forward to Gregg's first appointment and everything was going well. He completed the consultation form and I stepped out of the room to allow him to undress. Back in the treatment room, Gregg's toenails caught my attention immediately.

'Aphrodite's Pink Nightie,' Gregg said, noticing me staring.

'Sorry,' I croaked, caught off guard.

'The colour. It's Aphrodite's Pink Nightie. You like?'

What was I supposed to say? 'Yep, it really sets off your size 12 plates of meat.'

I opted for the more diplomatic, 'Lovely.'

'I'm not gay,' he said a little less convincingly than he had on the phone.

A full body wax can take a good couple of hours depending on how big, and how hairy, the client is. Gregg is about six feet tall, big built, and hairy, so he needed the full two hours. During this time, he talked at me like a Gatling gun, barely stopping for breath.

I heard all about his job as a top lawyer; his bitch ex-wife who got the dogs and the house and then spread rumours about him shagging his male boss; his new wife who didn't understand him; and his beautiful baby girl.

As the appointment went on, he loosened up, and nervously confessed to enjoying dressing as a woman. He admitted to leaving the nail varnish on to gauge my response. Reassured that I hadn't been judgemental, he felt he could be honest with me. His second wife, who is considerably younger than him, had been less open-minded when she discovered him wearing a dress and Hoovering the living room. *I* would have been more annoyed he was so cliched; Freddie Mercury was hoovering the living room dressed as a woman way back in 1984. If anything, it was detrimental to women's lib that he thought housework was synonymous with dressing as a woman.

The cork was out of the bottle, anyway, and when he arrived for his second appointment, Gregg was more camp than Elton John singing YMCA at the Eurovision Song Contest. He wanted to chat about the Kardashians and The Real Housewives of Atlanta; who wore what dress to the Oscars two weeks before; and what kind of foundation and mascara I use. All in all, he was more like my teenage daughter than my male client, but I like to think of my treatment room as a sanctuary of sorts, so I indulged him in letting off some of that pent-up frustration.

At the end of the appointment I stepped out to let him get dressed. As I do with all my clients, I told him to give me a shout when he was ready. A minute later he called me in and I opened the door to an image that at best unsettled me. Gregg was standing beside my treatment bed wearing high heels, fishnet stockings, a red lacy bra, and a pair of crotchless knickers.

'What do you think?' he asked, sashaying his hips.

I was speechless, distracted by his cock and balls, swinging loose between his legs.

Composing myself, I managed, 'Well, you didn't get them in Tesco, did you?' And eyed the knickers.

'I know, they're amazing, right,' he enthused, shaking his hips again.

Standing in front of me displaying his wares, he decided to ambush me and organise a double date: me and hubby, him and his wife Carrie. With hindsight I think he hypnotised me with his swinging cock, the result of shaking his hips so much. Using his member as a makeshift pocket-watch, I had become suggestible and agreed to dinner and a show.

Gregg was giddier than a child at Christmas, and started planning his outfit immediately. I was more interested in him getting back into the outfit he'd arrived in, and putting his plums away. Re-dressing in front of me, he gave me a peck on the cheek, and as he left asked me to make sure that hubby knew he wasn't gay.

I opted not to tell hubby anything. It's hard enough to get him to agree to go out socially at the best of times, so if I'd let him know that the guy we were going out with might turn up like Dr Frank-n-Furter, it would have been nigh on impossible. Not because he has anything against transvestites, he just doesn't like to be part of a scene when we're out.

As we were driving over to pick them up (hubby volunteered to drive, so that the rest of us could have a drink), I received a message from Gregg explaining that Carrie was tired and wouldn't be coming out with us. This made me nervous. I knew Carrie didn't like Gregg dressing as a woman, and I was worried it meant he would come running up the drive with his dick hanging out the bottom of a mini-skirt.

Thankfully, when he appeared, he was dressed very conservatively, but he did climb into the back of the car with a bag of drinks, screaming, 'Cocktails, bitches.'

I didn't even need to look at hubby to know he would struggle with the machine gun chatter coming from the back. Hubby can blether himself, but he is a quick judge of character and clearly figured there was no point trying to get into a conversation. He sat quietly and listened.

In the restaurant, Gregg kept going like a steam train of nonsense, and made hubby even more uneasy with the amount of touching going on. Every so often Gregg put his hand on hubby's arm or shoulder and said things like, 'How tall are you?' Then he began scrolling through his phone, sharing photos of himself in his pants with hubby, and commenting, 'This was me when I was deadlifting 200 kilos.' Hubby would patiently look up from his madras and mumble in acknowledgement, before returning to his dinner.

After dinner, we went to a show, during which hubby's boundaries were really pushed. He ended up sitting between Gregg and me, which I already knew would bother him as he'd have to make small talk at the interval. That turned out to be the least of his worries. Gregg decided to tell hubby about the time he ran the London marathon, which had resulted in him knackering his knees to the point that they needed to be replaced. Gregg illustrated the problem areas in the muscles above his knee, by rubbing his thumb and forefinger repeatedly up and down hubby's thigh. As hubby had his jacket on his lap, I was unable to see what was happening, but he told me later how Gregg was about three seconds and three inches away from being launched over the balcony.

Hubby asked me the next day, 'Does he know I'm not gay?'

And I replied, 'Yeah, but I don't think he knows that he *is*.'

Gregg has since asked if he and I can go out on the town for a girly day, with him as his alter ego Tabatha. I am reluctant, truth be told, for the same reason that he is keen. He thinks that if we go out together, people will just see us as two big women, whereas I think people will see us as two men in drag. I don't know if I'm ready for that.

On the plus side, at least I've finally got someone I can swap outfits with.

Chapter Twenty-Six

Tom

Vanity Profanity...

There are many reasons why someone may decide to get waxed: for hygiene purposes, sports, heightened sexual pleasure, or plain comfort. For some, it's just part of an overall beauty regimen that involves various treatments: fake tan, Botox, lip fillers, microblading, derma-peels, acrylic nails, hair extensions, IPL, facials, anal bleaching... the list goes on.

Most people are simply trying to be the best possible version of themselves: for their own self-worth, for their significant other, or even the person they would like to have as their significant other. For others, it fuels a grandiose image that they have of themselves, and the very worst of these are nothing short of narcissists.

In the pretence of some level of maturity in this book, let me give you a potted history of narcissism.

In Greek mythology, Narcissus was a hunter noted for his beauty. The son of a God and a nymph, so proud of his looks was he, he disdained those who loved him. Nemesis, a Goddess who enacted retribution against those who succumb to hubris, noticed his arrogance and attracted him to a pool in which he saw his own reflection. Falling in love with that, his own image, he was trapped, unable to leave the poolside, where losing the will to live, he withered and died. This led to the term narcissism, where someone is fixated by their appearance or public perception. (Legend has it that Narcissus liked a Brazilian and Nemesis preferred a Hollywood, but that could just be a myth.)

Apologies for the tenuous link to Greek mythology and waxing, you can thank hubby for that. I let him add that in, as he is almost as obsessed with Greek and Roman mythology as he is with stationery. Perhaps because both are full of strong rulers. He is currently in the corner of the room giggling to himself about how much Romulus and Remus's adopted mother could do with a good wax, whilst Googling what Icarus used to glue his wings together – hubby is almost certain it was wax.

I don't know what you call the opposite of narcissism, but whatever it is, hubby suffers from it. I remind him constantly to look in the mirror before he leaves the house, something which he rarely does, showing scant regard for his appearance.

He has a look, which he himself describes as, 'a fat Proclaimer', that is, a tubby version of twins Charlie and Craig Reid from Scottish folk/rock band The Proclaimers – as opposed to just a fat guy who makes announcements.

I won't lie, it's not a bad likeness. He even has the thick-rimmed glasses and unfortunate selection of shirts, ranging from medium to extra-extra-extra-extra-large, due to his fondness for yo-yo dieting. Twenty to thirty years ago, hubby's disregard for any notion of style or self-awareness would simply have labelled him a man's man. In today's more body conscious, fashion- driven world, he's more likely to be called a fat, badly-dressed, middle-aged man. And I wouldn't have him any other way. His happy-go-lucky attitude is far more attractive to me than a tight body and trendy clothes.

My client Tom, very much the antithesis of hubby, is a man so obsessed with his own image, he can lose an entire morning if he catches a glimpse of himself on a reflective surface. I'm sure you've encountered guys like Tom before, he's the guy in the gym who always positions himself in front of the mirror to admire his bulging muscles. Having spent years strengthening his body, he has done precious little to fortify his brain or personality. Conversations during Tom's appointments were a little like watching paint dry, whilst simultaneously drinking the left-over paint. If you're worried he might be offended by what I'm writing, don't worry, he will never read it – that would involve something other than preening himself in a mirror. I'm not entirely sure he can read, anyway. When I asked him to complete a consultation form, he just drew lots of little pictures of himself.

If you are sensing a level of anger towards Tom, that seems uncharacteristic with my mantra of 'find the funny', then you are right. He was the only client, other than the rapey one, and the Mummy Pimp, that I came close to asking not to come back. Fortunately, he emigrated to Australia which saved me the trouble. The reason for my anger was his horrific attitude towards women, who he believed should only be doing one of three things '...cooking my dinner, cleaning my house or polishing my knob.' Unbelievably, this twat has a wife who has had a child with him. Shortly after the baby was born hubby bumped into Tom and enquired as to how mummy and baby were. Tom's reply was that she had better get herself back to work soon, as she wasn't going to be spending his money. When hubby pointed out that his wife had just given birth to his child and could probably do with some time to recuperate and bond with the baby, it was met with, 'No excuse.'

The irony was that Tom had no money. As the youngest child of wealthy parents his lifestyle was funded by his mum and dad, who regularly bailed him out from one failed business venture after another. This included, but was not limited to: property development, car sales, clothes lines, and dabbling in a bit of 'green' – grown in his parents' sizeable greenhouse and completely without their knowledge,

One of Tom's appointments, I did thoroughly enjoy, and to date it probably ranks as one of my most favourite. I will get to that shortly but first, the back-story.

Tom had recently reinvented himself as a personal trainer. This arose from a misplaced belief that because he had spent a lot of time in the gym lifting weights, he could train other people to look like him. What he failed to consider was that he had injected enough steroids to chemically enhance the entire Russian Olympic team – not something you can advertise on your business cards. (On a side note, there was something else Tom didn't put on his business cards, which was his contact details, thus making them as ineffectual as his brain.)

His claim to be a professional personal trainer was somewhat bolstered by him having secured a position working for a well-known national gym chain. I was surprised such a company would take someone like Tom on, him being what you would call a fanny – trust me, I know a fanny when I see one – but that's when I learned something about these big-box gyms that blew my mind.

If you're not a member of such a gym, you may not know how they operate, so let me fill you in. As a member, you pay a fee to the gym and they allow you to use their facilities, which I'm sure you agree is a perfectly normal state of play for any organisation with paid membership. But did you know that the staff in the gym are also paying to be there? Not only that, but they are paying significantly more than the members. Yep, that's right, they are paying to go to work. They open and close the gym, man the desk, and keep everything squared away, whilst paying for the privilege.

Whoever came up with that as a business model is nothing short of a genius. For hundreds of years, it has been accepted that if you do a job for someone, they pay you money and everyone is happy. Then in the twenty first century someone said, 'Wait a minute, what if as well as making the customers pay, we make the staff pay too?'

I imagine there were people who told that person he was dreaming, it would be impossible, nobody would pay to come to work. But he dared to dream and now thanks to him, up and down the country there are hundreds of muscular men and women paying to go to work. The thinking is that the personal trainers get the members to sign up for PT sessions at an additional cost, and that is how they make their money.

(Wait, I've just realised this isn't a new business model at all, pimps have been doing it for years – taking a cut from people selling their bodies. Keep your eyes peeled for my next book: Pimps, Prostitutes and Personal Trainers – From Johns to Gyms.)

So, Tom was whoring himself out to the big gym-box, but ever the fanny, he saw an opportunity too good to miss. His golden ticket was protein powder – because as all good steroid-fuelled meatheads know, you need to make a show of getting your protein in, otherwise people might think you are on steroids.

His plan was to, 'buy cheap in bulk, mark it up and make a tidy profit selling it to the members.' When he told me his 'bulletproof' plan, I pointed out that you can buy protein powder in Tesco. This baffled Tom and prompted the simple response of, 'So?'

'So, I think Tesco's idea of buying in bulk is going to be significantly more substantial than yours. That means they get it cheaper, allowing them to sell it cheaper,' I explained.

Unperturbed by my dose of common sense, he borrowed five thousand pounds from his parents and placed an order with a South African company for one ton of unpackaged protein powder. The money cleared his account before he considered where and how to store the protein, how to package it, and how to distribute it. Not that this was an issue, as the lovely African man he was dealing with agreed to keep the protein safe in his warehouse in Africa. Apparently, Tom was unaware that as the protein was intended to be ingested, it had a shelf life the same way that any food stuff would. Months passed, and the protein was still slowly degrading in Africa.

Tom was advised to rent a refrigerated unit to store the powder in before arranging for the delivery. Having priced the cost of such a unit, he opted instead to rent a wooden crate in a local self-storage warehouse – far more cost effective, yet wholly unfit for purpose. He purchased packaging emblazoned with a company name and logo that he (that is, his parents) had paid to be professionally designed.

Finally, nearly a year after having purchased his protein, he was ready to accept delivery. Imagine Tom's surprise when he phoned his supplier and was told that to secure delivery he needed to make a further payment of £1800. This confused Tom as he had been told that delivery was included in the initial £5000, but he was reassured when the nice man explained that it was just to pay for the courier's insurance, and he would get £1700 back upon receipt.

If you are wondering what that noise is in your head, it is alarm bells, which is good because it means you are not an imbecile. An ordinary garden-variety idiot would realise what was happening at this point and walk away. Not Tom.

After hitting his parents up for another £1800 he went to the Post Office to wire transfer the money. If you are thinking he couldn't get any thicker, then brace yourself. The woman at the Post Office refused to transfer the money, explaining that she was trained to spot scams in order to protect vulnerable customers, and she was certain that this situation fitted the criteria.

Ding-ding-ding-ding-ding the alarm bells squeal, but undeterred, Tom went to a less reputable establishment who happily transferred the money for a larger fee. Having confirmed the payment with his dealer (what else would you call a man who supplies you with white powder), he went back to dreaming of being the next Joe Wickes.

Fast forward to my treatment room, with Tom flat on his back, soles of his feet together, and knees apart as I waxed his balls. His phone, permanently attached to his hand for the seemingly endless selfies, started ringing, with, 'Bitch Betta Have My Money' by Tyga, blasting out. Well, what else would a middle-class, white guy have as his ring-tone?

Holding his index finger up towards me, indicating I should stop talking, he answered the call. It didn't take long for me to work out that it was Africa calling, and Tom wasn't happy. It turned out the protein hadn't been loaded on to a cargo plane as expected, and it would take a further payment of £2000, or it never would. I swear I could hear the penny drop when Tom finally worked out that there was no protein, there never had been and there never would be.

He leapt off the treatment bed in a rage and stormed up and down the room, the vascularity in his bulging arms and legs seeming less impressive as his little steroid willy jiggled about. He put the phone on speaker so he could hold it in front of himself and scream obscenities at the screen. It probably sounded more frightening than it looked, because it is very difficult to look intimidating when you are wearing white ankle socks and no pants. When Tom paused for breath the man on the other end took his opportunity, and in the thickest South African accent I have ever heard, said, 'Fuck you, stupid', and hung up. Purely out of professionalism I didn't laugh, at least not until Tom left, which was bloody hard, especially as he insisted that I finish the wax whilst he lay there with tears in his eyes.

Oh, and just in case you were waiting for an answer, hubby has confirmed it was wax that Icarus used to make his wings. And if you are the kind of person who believes Icarus and his father were able to fly, then I know a guy who will sell you a ton of protein cheap.

CHAPTER TWENTY-SEVEN

Nicholas

ROBOCOCK...

Even after all my years waxing, it never fails to amaze me when I come across something new, particularly when it comes to people's sexual proclivities.

With the cross section of clients that I have, I genuinely believed I'd heard pretty much everything, but you're never too old to learn. Even when you get to my gran's age, every day's a school day.

This was highlighted recently when I had occasion to correct Gran after I heard her telling her friend all about 'felching'.

'It's a cross between farting and belching,' she confidently told her eighty-two-year old pal.

I so wish she was right, but she wasn't, and while I desperately didn't want to tell her the truth, I had to stop her from using the word in public. I tried to explain it was actually a lot ruder than that and she shouldn't use it ever again. If anything, that just made her more inquisitive; she started badgering me for an explanation.

'Mona, Patricia and I have a combined age of one hundred and sixty, I doubt very much you could possibly tell us anything we haven't heard before,' she snapped.

'Okay then, Gran, felching is when a man ejaculates in an orifice, usually the anus, before sucking the ejaculate back out using his mouth, often then kissing his partner. It's a practice usually associated with gay men,' I snapped back, in an exaggerated whisper.

Patricia let out an involuntary gasp and put her hand to her mouth.

'That is just filth, Mona. You should be ashamed of yourself,' Gran shot back.

'It's not me who's loudly using the word in Debenham's café, though, is it Gran?' I laughed, and she looked around sheepishly to see if anyone had heard her.

Gran's disgust was purely an act for Patricia's benefit, I can assure you; her language had remained blue since Grampa passed. I think she reached an all-time low when talking to her niece, the daughter of 'the old C who was whoring about town'. On that occasion it was the old C's husband, her niece's father, who was getting it,

Gran does not like her brother-in-law, not one little bit, which is understandable because like his wife, he is a bit of an arse. Their daughter, however, is one of those people everybody loves, and despite technically being my father's cousin the whole family knows her as Auntie Jan.

Auntie Jan joined Gran, hubby, the kids and me for dinner in a local restaurant, where my gran, Jan, and myself indulged in a little too much wine. Hubby, ever the sensible one, was driving, so stuck to soft drinks. After the meal we all went back to Gran's, where the drinkers retired to the dining room to keep drinking, and hubby and the kids went to the living room to fall asleep in front of the telly. Auntie Jan's dad had been taken into hospital a few days earlier with a head injury, supposedly the result of a fall. Uncle Johnny was frequently admitted to hospital following 'falls'; in truth he and Aunt Kath would get drunk and batter each other. Something which, according to Auntie Jan, they had done for as long as she could remember.

Having discussed the issue at length, now the kids were out of earshot, Gran had a thought she wanted to share with us. Please bear in mind that this is something said by a seventy-seven-year-old woman to her fifty-eight-year-old niece about her ninety-year-old father. I heard it first hand and I still can't believe it.

'The problem with your dad, Jan, is that he's a wanker. He's probably happy he's in hospital, so that he's away from your mother and can have a wank in peace. He'll be sat in that bed wanking away, eating Rich Tea biscuits, and when the doctor comes to do his rounds with his students and asks if there is anything he needs, he'll tell him, "Yeah, peace to have a wank".'

I was so shocked I couldn't even laugh. It was the Rich Tea biscuits that really threw me. Looking at Auntie Jan I could see she was just as gobsmacked.

Amazingly, when I regaled hubby with the story later he had his own story that involved Rich Tea biscuits and masturbating.

When he was a teenager, a group of boys living in his neighbourhood played a game they imaginatively entitled 'Risk It For A Biscuit'. The game involved standing in a circle and masturbating and when they were ready, ejaculating onto a Rich Tea biscuit. The last person to come had to eat the biscuit.

In an even more disgusting turn of events, one of the guys, who was sick of always losing, had taken to pissing on the biscuit as he could never finish quickly enough. Unfortunately, his plan backfired, and he was immediately disqualified and forced to eat a Piss Jizz Biscuit – keep your eyes peeled for the McVities version the Cumstard Cream, coming to a supermarket aisle near you soon.

I would like to tell you it was understandable because this was a different time, before the internet and smartphones, when young people had nothing better to do with their time. But there is no excuse for that level of depravity, even in cave man times. Besides which, I was baffled this was even public knowledge. If there was ever a group that shouldn't have been discussing their activities with the wider community, then surely it would be Wank Club?

The first rule of Wank Club is: Do Not Talk About Wank Club.

Having now met a couple of members of Wank Club – who, worryingly, are parents at the kids' school – I understand how the secret got out. I don't think it would be unfair to say that the biscuit was by far the most intelligent member of the group.

On the subject of weird things that men do with their penises, let me seamlessly segue into one of my most recent lessons in willy weirdness.

A new client, Nicholas, had phoned me to enquire about male waxing, and having discussed the treatment he decided to book in. Towards the end of the call he casually explained that he wore a cock cage and asked if that would be a problem, explaining that his girlfriend kept the key, so he couldn't remove it.

I didn't want to admit to him I didn't know what the hell a cock cage was, or indeed whether it would be a problem. Without committing to anything, I played it cool and told him I would need to look at it first to determine if it would be an issue. Happy with my response, he confirmed the booking details and ended the call.

Later that day I asked hubby if he knew what a cock cage was, and a look of alarm spread across his face.

'I'm not wearing a bloody cock cage,' he shrieked.

And only once I assured him he wasn't going to be wearing one would he give me brief description of what a cock cage was.

Unsurprisingly, it is literally a cage that a guy puts his cock in, which is then locked, and the key is held by a third party, usually his partner. Hubby explained that the purpose was to prevent the wearer from getting an erection, thus preventing them from being able to orgasm. Although helpful, this wasn't vivid enough for me to imagine exactly this strange contraption, let alone gauge how easy it would be to wax around it.

A Google image search both filled in the holes in my imagination and served to raise more questions. The cage itself can be made from different materials including metal, silicone, and leather, and comes in various styles – certainly a lot more stylish than the wrought iron penis prison I had in my head. What I wasn't expecting were the optional extras, like a urethral plug (a metal bar that gets pushed down inside the penis) and an attached butt plug (it's a real pain in the ass).

Best case scenario, I was looking at a simple leather banana hammock, secured behind the testicles with a small padlock. Worst case scenario, I was looking at a full metal enclosure with penis and butt inserts, like a genital Robocop, but with a thatch of hair like an 80's Scouser. Given that Nicholas had booked in to have everything removed, that could be a problem.

There are few appointments I get nervous about, but this was one of them. I have no problems dealing with penises, it's simply part of the job, but I had never seen one dressed like a medieval knight, perhaps, Richard the Lionheart. (Side-note: Richard was King of England from 1189-1199. And to prove to hubby, who is still unsure about whether I can make a book about waxing people's bits, informative and mature, let me point out we have now covered the gestation period of human beings, Greek mythology and English history. At the risk of sounding arrogant I think I may be a modern-day Jane Austen.)

Anyway, all I could do was wait in trepidation for King Dick, and deep-clean my laptop search history in case the kids stumbled across images of the Oxballs Atomic Jock Stretchy – £34.99 from Lovehoney.

All the worry turned out to be for nothing as Nicholas was sporting a basic leather number, which left most of the pubic area exposed. I've never been so happy to see an unplugged butthole; I nearly clapped when he got on all fours.

During the appointment he explained that he was a submissive, and his girlfriend was his dom. She controlled when he could have sex or masturbate, deliberately putting him in situations where he would get aroused, so the leather restraint would squash his willie. One of her favourite activities was have lesbian sex whilst he watched, and she screamed horrible things at him about being a maggot and such. I was very much picking up that she was way more into it than Nicholas. Perhaps he was tricked into it when he heard her say something about 'lesbian sex' without paying proper attention. The next thing he knew his todger had been placed on remand with no chance of parole.

Nicholas also seemed rather downbeat about his wax treatment, telling me towards the end of the appointment that his other half wanted him smooth, so she could upgrade his hardware. He was going full metal jacket but fortunately wasn't getting anything shoved inside him, not yet anyway.

My experience with Nicholas made me wonder how many people have found themselves in the BDSM world by accident? And once they were in too deep, just accepted they were now a full-time gimp, living in a cupboard under the stairs, like a leather-clad Harry Potter adorned with a ball-gag.

Nicholas only came for one appointment, cancelling his second because he and his girlfriend were moving to Amsterdam – which we all know is the home of normal. As much as I am all for freedom of choice and everyone's right to live as they see fit, some things are just plain weird. And I would argue that allowing someone to hold your genitals to ransom is one step away from being a plotline in Game of Thrones.

For the record it wasn't a client who told me about felching, it was hubby. *And* he seemed oddly knowledgeable about cock cages. I'm not entirely certain the he wasn't a founding member of the Wank Club either. I have a horrible feeling he might be the one who pissed on the biscuit.

Chapter Twenty-Eight

Harvey

What a review...

Today most businesses need to have an 'online presence', even if they don't trade online. This has largely been driven by people's thirst for online reviews, which has quickly become the modern word of mouth.

Consumers want to know as much as they can about a business before they spend a penny. This has led to a multitude of review sites, from TripAdvisor to Revoo, Yelp to Trustpilot – whether you are looking to book a hotel or buy a book, you can find a review online.

Although it can be useful to have access to people's opinions of products and services, you must remember to take them with a pinch of salt. Remember that reviews are generally written by people, and if you have ever met people, you will know that a lot of them are crazy. Beyond that, people often have an agenda – great reviews written by the company themselves or dreadful reviews written by their competitors. Worse still, reviews are often fake. There are companies who, for a fee, will provide you with hundreds of glowing reviews from fake accounts of non-existent people. This practice is being countered by many of the big sites, making it more difficult for businesses to peddle 'fake news' (I can now only ever read those words in the voice of President Trump, which, given the current topic, is ironic. If a business had received the number of negative reviews that he has, they would have folded in the first week. He on the other hand is oblivious. I don't know where that man's self-confidence comes from, but it is astonishing).

Hubby is a little more traditional when it comes to reviews, he feels that online feedback is a little impersonal, preferring the relatively old-fashioned method of pen and paper. When I pointed out that writing a review in a letter, which is then posted to the person that the review is about, isn't really reaching the target market the way it should, it fell on deaf ears. You, of course, will have probably worked out this is just another way of fuelling his tragic passion for stationery. I know this, because in all the years we have been together he has written a grand total of zero letters, either positive or negative. Which is in stark contrast to both the number of letters he said he was going to write, somewhere around four and a half thousand I reckon (he is very vocal about good and bad service but has no follow-through), and the amount of writing paper and pens he has bought.

Outside of school and large offices I had never encountered a stationery cupboard before – until hubby. His was meant to be a cupboard for cleaning stuff, mops/brushes, Hoover, etc., but bit by bit he has turned it into a mini Rymans. *In our house.* That's who I am married to. Did you know there is a national stationery show? It is billed as a two-day stationery extravaganza, and I wish that I didn't know that.

I first encountered hubby's bizarre combination of gushing enthusiasm yet crushing procrastination towards written feedback, following a test drive of a Toyota Yaris. The salesman at the car dealership was a young guy with a pleasant, laidback attitude, and buckets of patter. Exactly the kind of personality that lends itself to selling things to people, especially gullible people whose heads are easily turned.

The way that hubby went on about him on the drive home I thought he was going to phone and ask him out on a date. We didn't even buy the bloody car because it was only a three-door, and as I was pregnant we wanted a five-door. Incidentally, we were trading in hubby's 'sports car'. If you think that a man who collects headed notepaper is too boring to have a sports car, then you are partially right. From the outside it looked and sounded like a sports car, but on the inside, it had fake walnut trim and a beige velour interior. Imagine a nursing home lounge that could do nought-to-sixty in five seconds and you're in the right area.

Regardless of the salesman's inability to sell us a car, hubby was going to be writing a letter to his boss to tell him what a 'lovely young man' he was. Hubby himself was only twenty-four at the time, physically anyway. Mentally he was nudging seventy.

Despite his good intentions, he never got around to writing that letter. Or any letter, to my knowledge – I think he would have an anxiety attack if he had to rip one sheet of paper out of his beloved writing pads. He prefers to keep supermarket receipts in his wallet, so that he can write notes on them, if need be.

Fortunately, my clients leave reviews for me on Facebook, which is my preferred method of interacting with the wider world, as opposed to people sending me handwritten notes about how much they enjoy their baldy fanny – which would serve no purpose other than to freak me out.

At the time of writing, I am proud to say I have a solid five-star rating, and I can assure you that none of the feedback is fake. Each review on my page has been written by someone whose genitals I have personally seen. I can't see that becoming an effective method of confirming authenticity – being able to accurately describe the fanny of the person who has left the review – but I *could*, that's all I'm saying. Maybe something for Trustpilot to think about going forward.

Although I have an impeccable online record, my worst review was delivered first hand in my very own place of work.

One wet Tuesday morning, I started work late after attending a school assembly for our youngest child, only managing to squeeze four clients in before taking a break for lunch. Leaving my treatment room, I went in to the toilet to grab a tissue to blow my nose, only to be greeted with a massive turd in the middle of the floor, right in front of the sink. As far as reviews go, shitting on the floor sends a very loud, clear message.

It stank, but more shocking than the smell, was the realisation that it must have been one of *my* four clients who had shat on the floor, as hubby hadn't had any that day. I mentally flicked through the list of suspects in a game of Guess Who? Or should that be Guess Poo?

By the way, other well-known family board games that can also be used for that joke are – Monplopoly, Mouse Crap, Poodo (Cluedo – arguably more of an audible one), Battleshit or at a real push, Scrapple. Take your pick. They're all equally childish, but I would plump for Monplopoly because I think it is cleverer than the others. You need to think about it for a second before you realise plop is in there, I haven't just misspelled Monopoly.

Back to the list of suspects – all in their mid-fifties and all well to do. My mind boggled (Boggle – another game that almost made the list due to the word bog being in the title. But given that the perpetrator had missed the bog with their offering, it never made it. I couldn't help myself, though, because the word makes me giggle). I couldn't imagine any of them deliberately taking a shit on my floor. Outside of primary schools, student bars and nursing homes, *where* would you find people who arbitrarily take a dump on the floor?

Once the initial shock passed, I put on a pair of latex gloves, fashioned a makeshift catcher's mitt out of rolled up toilet paper and scooped up the jobbie (a favourite word of my gran's, who is Scottish: noun; jobbie (plural jobbies) 1. (vulgar) a piece of shit.)

Even through the wad of toilet paper I could feel the soft faeces yield to my grasp, like Plasticine that had been well handled. It dropped with a plop into the toilet, a splash of water landing on my flip-flopped foot and making me retch.

It left me with a dilemma. Should I contact the ladies I had waxed that morning, to try and ascertain who the culprit was, or did I chalk it up to 'shit happens'.

Curiosity got the better of me and I decided to do a little digging, not easy, given how delicate the matter was. You can't just straight out ask someone if they shat on your floor, because no matter how sensitively you approach the topic you're still suggesting you think they're capable of curling one off on your floor. Imagine that for a second, if someone you knew told you that you looked like the kind of person who would shit on a bathroom floor. It's impossible to put a positive spin on that. So I opted for a more tactful approach, sending them all the following text message:

Hi ladies, I've just found a leak in the bathroom of my treatment room. Trying to figure out how long it has been leaking for, did anyone notice anything this morning? xx

My softly, softly approach worked better than I could have hoped, with three of the ladies telling me they hadn't used the bathroom so unfortunately, they couldn't help. That only left Linda, who confirmed that she had used the loo but hadn't noticed a leak. It must have started sometime after her appointment, she suggested.

Of the four of them, I would have picked Linda as the least likely to have committed a shit and run. She had recently taken early retirement from her post as a head teacher of a local primary school, in order to travel the world with her husband, who was ten years older and a retired banker. They had an idyllic life, living in a beautiful cottage in the countryside, which they moved to when their kids had flown the nest. When they weren't travelling, they were both heavily involved with the church and various associated groups.

Despite her serious job, religious beliefs, and staid appearance, she was far from prudish and she liked a laugh. But she couldn't abide toilet humour (a throwback to her years in education teaching children who find nothing funnier than farting), which is what made her seem even less plausible as the culprit.

The super-sleuths amongst you may already be picking holes in my investigation but don't worry, I may not be Miss Marple, but I am a mum, so it's not easy to pull the wool over my eyes. Just because Linda admitted using the bathroom doesn't mean one of the other ladies wasn't lying. Let's be honest, if you are willing to shit on the floor, then you are certainly willing to lie about it.

I knew it had to be Linda, though, as she had been my last client that morning and she had admitted to using the bathroom. Therefore, if it wasn't her, it must have happened earlier, and she would have seen the evidence when she used the bathroom. If that was the case, when I asked her if she had seen a leak, I would fully expect her to say, 'No I didn't, but I did see a steaming turd.' Or words to that effect.

To be fair, if she had seen it, I would have expected her to mention it at the start of her appointment. I certainly would if I saw a crap on the floor in a bathroom I was using, if only just to make sure no one suspected me of carrying out the dirty protest.

Your average person might have left it at that, having satisfied their curiosity as to who the perpetrator was. But like a faecal Sherlock Holmes, I wanted justice, I had to get Linda to confess and explain herself. In my head, I had no other option than to phone her and secure a confession. It was a difficult conversation. Not the most difficult conversation I have ever had, but very close. Let me give you the gist of it:

Me: 'Hi, Linda, how are you?'

Linda: 'Oh, hi, Mona. I'm good thanks, is everything okay? Did I leave something behind at my appointment?'

Me: 'Well, you could say that. Was everything alright when you used the bathroom at mine today?'

L: 'Yes, everything was fine. There definitely wasn't a leak, though, sorry I can't be of more help, Mona.'

Me: 'Oh that's fine, there isn't actually a leak. Can I ask, did you have an accident in the bathroom, Linda?'

L: 'An accident? What like a fall? No.'

Me: 'No, not a fall. Look, there is no easy way to say this, so I'll just come out with it. Did you do a poo on the bathroom floor?'

L: 'Jesus Christ, of course I didn't shit on your floor. (Not very Christian of her I thought, using the Lord's name in vain alongside profanity. This is certainly the kind of behaviour I would expect from a floor crapper.) What's wrong with you, Mona?'

Me: 'I'm sorry, Linda, but it could only be you who did it as nobody used the bathroom after you. I just want to know, why? Is everything alright at home? I know some people struggle to adjust to retirement, particularly early retirement.'

L: 'So, let me get this straight. You think I'm struggling to fill my time now I'm retired, so have taken to shitting on bathroom floors. Really, Mona?'

Me: 'Let's not get worked up. I just wanted to give you a call and let you know I'm here if you need me. You know, if you need to speak to anyone about anything.'

I came off the phone seething. The audacity of the woman. First, she shits on my floor and then not only does she deny it, but she also tries to make me feel bad about calling her out. I stormed into the house, ready to vent about it to hubby.

As I stomped into the kitchen, before I could even open my mouth, without even looking up from his laptop he piped up with, 'You had a little visitor in your workroom this morning.'

This immediately took the wind out of my sails.

'What do you mean?' I asked.

'Harvey, from next door,' he replied. 'Your last client must have left the door open; he was coming out of the toilet when I went in to get my laptop from the office. Maybe he was thirsty.' He chuckled to himself.

Harvey is our next-door neighbour's Cocker Spaniel, who occasionally wanders into our garden. And with that piece of information you don't need to be Columbo to work out who shit on the floor.

If only I had spoke to hubby first, I wouldn't have had what was the most difficult conversation of my life: phoning Linda back to apologise.

Fortunately, she saw the funny side and even brought a packet of poo bags to her next appointment.

Chapter Twenty-Nine

Joanne

Guess who's coming to dinner...

Food glorious food. Never a truer word has been spoken, than when little Oliver sang about the wonder of food. Oliver Twist that is, not Oliver Hardy, who my gran insisted sang the song. I am beginning to genuinely worry about her, I think she may be drinking too much Merlot.

When it comes to food, hubby and I go all out. If we exercised with the commitment with which we ate, we would both be competing at the Olympic games. In multiple events. For me, I think the over-indulgence is a throwback to my neglected childhood. My father would always be fed first and best, then my sisters and I got the scraps. Often my mother wouldn't even go to the bother of cooking for us. One of her favourite tricks was to leave a can of beans on the radiator till it was warm, and then let us eat them straight out of the tin. It's hard to tell if she was a crappy mum or a progressive thinker being environmentally friendly. No gas was wasted in heating the beans or water used in washing the dishes; some may say she was a visionary. The word I would use rhymes with James Hunt. Granted, it may have been better than the gruel little Oliver was forced to eat, but only marginally. And at least he got a bowl.

For hubby, it is fair to say his over-indulgence is down to being a greedy bastard. This may seem harsh, but it is true, and he admits it. Nothing annoys him more than when people tell him he's not fat – he openly says he is clinically obese, only to be told back that he is mistaken. It's an odd response. It's clear to look at him that he *is* fat, and he embraces it. To try and tell him otherwise is akin to Samuel L Jackson telling someone he is black and them trying to convince him that he isn't.

Those of you who have been paying attention may be thinking, 'Wait a minute, didn't he lose weight when he became aware that his arse might collapse?' And yes, you are right, he did. But such is his desire to cram food down his throat, he ultimately decided it was worth the risk.

Although we both display, what I can only describe as a shameful level of gluttony, I can at least claim to be a little more discerning than my garbage can of a husband. He will eat anything, and by that I don't mean he will give most things a go, I mean he will eat anything that is put down in front of him. For him food is more than something to be enjoyed, it is a challenge. A challenge that can usually be split into two groups: quantity or novelty.

We eat out a lot, it is our real indulgence. We don't spend a lot of money on designer clothes or expensive hobbies, but we like to get our eat on. And if we go to a new restaurant that has either something strange or a 'challenge' on the menu, then I know what hubby is going to order. It is a compulsion, even if he doesn't fully comprehend what he is ordering, he needs to have it. This led to him inadvertently eating live eels when on holiday; he had mistaken them for beansprouts. The language barrier meant we were unclear if they were supposed to be cooked, but we didn't find out what they were until they were already swimming in his belly.

Sometimes, hubby creates food challenges that don't exist anywhere other than his head. We were enjoying a rare child-free morning at a local restaurant once, when the waitress mentioned in passing that no-one had ever ordered their largest cooked breakfast. What he heard was, 'I bet you can't eat our largest cooked breakfast.'

It was a monstrosity. Basically, they had taken the largest breakfast they offered and doubled it. This, I am sure, was done for a laugh and I doubt they ever expected anyone would be stupid enough to order it.

So, he ordered it. Despite having said on the way there that he only fancied a bacon roll. Out it came, on two plates. Full size dinner plates, that is, not one dinner plate and a side plate. I could tell he was in trouble early on, less than half way through his brow was slick with sweat. With each bite his breathing became more laboured, but he pushed on.

And when he laid his cutlery side-by-side on the empty plate, which was stacked on top of the other empty plate, he didn't look in the slightest bit victorious. He was a man with regret in his eyes, masked slightly by budding tears, and this was before we found out that the chef had broadcast his attempt.

Yes, unbeknown to us, after cooking, the chef put a photo of hubby's breakfast on Facebook with the comment, 'Some guy at my work has just ordered this – he's got no chance!'

When the waitress came to clear the table, she commented on how peaky hubby looked. This apparently dented the cave-man part of his ego, and in a bizarre and unnecessary attempt to prove his 'manliness' he said, 'Not at all. As a matter of fact, I'll have a piece of carrot cake and a gingerbread latte, please.'

Before we address the lunacy of a man who is on the cusp of vomiting his breakfast all over the table, choosing to order more food, can we take a moment to appreciate *what* he chose to order to cement his place in the annals of testosterone-fu-elled manhood.

The Vikings, the Romans, the Mongol Hordes, the Spartans are just some of the famous warriors from days gone by. They conquered continents, their enemies falling at their swords. And I think I am right in saying that the one thing they all have in common, is that they celebrated a successful battle with a nice bit of carrot cake and a gingerbread latte.

Hubby appeared so ill, the waitress glanced at me as if to say, 'Are you going to allow this?' I rolled my eyes and gave her the look that all women know only too well. Once she was clear he was an idiot, she brought him his coffee and cake. He gagged on every bite and slurp, but he finished it and sat there, greyer than John Major, with a smug little look on his face.

I hate to sound sexist, but this is another clear difference between men and women, because hubby is not alone. You look at any food challenge, and more often than not, you will find a sweaty, nauseous man.

When they were in their late teens one of hubby's friends boasted that he could beat the world hot dog eating record, which at the time stood at fifty hot dogs in twelve minutes. He claimed he could easily do fifty-four. This got the group so excited that they abandoned a night out, leaving the pub to go to a twenty-four-hour Tesco, where hubby bought sixty hot dogs and buns.

They went back to his parent's house and began cooking in earnest. His friend managed six and then vomited in the back garden. In his defence, he did make the bizarre decision to wash each one down with a glass of milk.

That was nearly twenty years ago, yet hubby's friend is regularly reminded of his failure. Nothing is mentioned of his time playing basketball for the national team or the trophies he achieved, but they frequently take the piss out of the time he vomited in a bush.

I appreciate not all men behave in this manner and I certainly don't want to stereotype half the population, but I bet *you* know a guy who can't be trusted in a restaurant.

Let me give you the most extreme example of bad behaviour at the dinner table I have ever heard of, and an equally extreme way of dealing with it.

I hadn't seen my client Joanne, the dominatrix, for over a year, which was strange because she usually visited the area at least every six months to see family.

I just assumed she was so busy buggering politicians with root vegetables, she had found a new waxer in London. As you may expect, the truth was far stranger.

I bumped into Joanne in Tesco – on an unconnected note the same Tesco that hubby and his crew bought the hot dogs from twenty years previously, which made me randomly think that maybe if he had spent less time playing sausages with his friends back then, he wouldn't have been a virgin when we met.

Joanne was surprised to see me and apologised profusely for not getting in touch. She was reassuring that she hadn't cheated on me with another waxer but due to an extraordinary situation, she had been shaving instead. Joanne is no stranger to peculiar requests and more often than not is able to accommodate them, however, it turned out there was one request she had – til now – always refused.

Several of her clients were turned on by the thought of being dominated by a hairy woman, which was at odds with most of her client base, who preferred a hair free dom. This latter struck me as strange, because if you are the kind of man who likes to get kicked in the balls repeatedly, would you really care if the kicker had waxed their legs? Then again, it's probably a damning indictment of how bizarre my own life is, that I'm questioning the hairiness of the kicker, not the desire to be kicked in the balls.

Enough of Joanne's clients had submitted requests to be battered by Chewbacca, that she felt she was missing out on a substantial sum of money. So, she hatched a plan and pitched it to those clients in pursuit of the hirsute.

I am far too amused with myself for coming up with that. It sounds good, though, doesn't it? I can see it as a Channel 5 game show, 'In Pursuit of the Hirsute', where teams of investigators chase hairy people across the country as they try to evade capture. We could get Rylan Clark-Neal to host it and the winner gets free waxing for life. The loser needs to spend the rest of their life living in Epping Forest as a tourist attraction.

Joanne suggested that once every four to six weeks she would host a dinner party for those clients who were aroused by a Hairy Mary, where she would be dressed only in her underwear. By not waxing or shaving over the four-week period she could see her no-hair-don't-care clients at the start of the month, and the Hair Bears at the end.

Unbelievably, they all went for it. So, roughly once a month she hosts an S&M version of Come Dine With Me, where a group of ten middle-aged men wearing nothing but masquerade masks, all sit round her dinner table for their tea. She struts up and down in nothing but her bra and pants and a thick coat of hair (she is particularly hairy, even for a Wookie), whilst dishing out both a lovely home-cooked meal and violent punishments for anyone who misbehaves.

In Joanne's case, examples of poor table etiquette include speaking when not spoken to, forgetting to say please and thank you, dropping food on the floor, and getting an erection at the table. Punishments for misbehaviour include open palm slaps to the face and body, scratches, nipple gripples, having a hairy armpit rubbed in your face, punches to the balls, and depending on what course they are on – a soup ladle to the dick.

These are men wealthy enough to pay Joanne's considerable fees, so we can assume they are successful in their working lives. Yet, once a month they sit naked around a table, with nine other naked men, and get the shit kicked out them. For fun. I dare you to find me a table of ten naked women paying for that kind of deranged service. You won't.

Joanne's biggest complaint about the evening is all the cooking involved, particularly as her calibre of client is used to fine dining – albeit usually clothed in Savile Row's finest and not just a mask and a stiffy.

On the plus side, at least she now has a use for all her leftover carrots.

Chapter Thirty

Mandy

Dyb, dyb, dyb...

It may seem that my client base is assembled from the characters of The Greatest Showman but most of them are very normal. The problem with that is, it doesn't make for very interesting reading.

Mandy is one of those clients. She is a wife and mother, and with her work as a renal nurse, an absolute angel. But as wonderful and lovely as she is, she is very normal. There are no weird sexual predilections that she has ever told me about, no drama with her husband or kids, and although her work is important, it isn't shocking.

She has never missed an appointment or turned up late, her personal hygiene is impeccable, and she doesn't as much as gossip about a single soul.

Yet, she has made the cut and taken her place here alongside the faecal-fanciers, cross-dressers and dick-kickers.

And the reason she has made it into such esteemed company, is because she is responsible for something that not only affected hubby for two years of his life, but also caused me to laugh so hard I nearly died.

Mandy was, at the time, the Beaver Akela of the local Boy Scouts group. For those of you not familiar with the Scout movement, let me briefly explain what that means, without putting you to sleep. Each Scout group is split into Beavers, Cubs, Scouts and Explorer Scouts. Beavers being the youngest, aged between 6-8 years old and Explorers the oldest, aged 14-18 years old. Each group is led by adult leaders, with the title of Akela given to the head leader.

During one of her appointments, Mandy mentioned that she could get my son's name pushed up the waiting list if he fancied going to Beavers. He was due to turn six the following week and at that time the waiting list was six months long. Most parents in the town would put their son's name down months, sometimes over a year, in advance of them turning six. I say *son*, because in the progressive town that we live in, at the turn of the century only boys were welcomed into the Scout pack, if you were a girl you could go to the Brownies and learn how to cook and sew. Which is only fair, because it is only the twenty-first century after all. This has changed now,

I hasten to add, and girls are welcomed, which was a difficult transition for some of the older leaders, who had never talked to girls before.

I thanked Mandy and took her up on the offer. Hubby wasn't thrilled when I told him, as he had briefly been a Cub at the same group – a long time before, obviously, when he was a child; he didn't have a breakdown and join as a grown man. The reason for his brief attendance was that one of the more psychotic Cubs decided he and hubby were going to play dodgeball with an innovative twist. Instead of a ball, hubby would have to dodge a chair that was being flung at his head. And when I say chair, I mean an old-fashioned school chair. For those of you under thirty you may not remember the classic metal-framed school chair with a solid wood seat and back. It was constructed so well you could sail it into battle. If you could stack and lift any more than two at a time you were classed as the school strongman.

In testament to the Scouts' rough and ready attitude of the time, when hubby complained to one of the leaders he was told, 'Well, you best get dodging then.'

That is exactly the staggering lack of adult intervention that led to hubby's tormentor eventually ending up in jail for attempted murder. In the interest of clarity, the charge was in no way connected to hubby, or indeed dodgeball. It was a rather vicious attack in a taxi rank on a Saturday night.

Anyway, Mandy managed to secure a place for our son a week after his birthday. Hubby and I took him along to the Scout hut for his first night and left him amidst a scene reminiscent of Lord of the Flies. And when we returned to collect him, Mandy asked all the parents to come into the hall, so she could make an announcement.

Thirty six-year-old Beavers were standing in a circle facing each other, in a vain attempt to control them. Some were so wired they were shaking on the spot. Mandy and the two other leaders looked shattered. Worryingly, for a woman who is used to arduous shifts lasting over twelve hours, she looked like these kids had ruined her in ninety minutes.

Her announcement was more of a plea. With the beleaguered look of an Akela on the edge, she asked for volunteers to be parent helpers, explaining that they were restricted to activities in the Scout hall if they couldn't get additional support. She tried to make it sound more appealing by pointing out that if ten parents volunteered, it would mean each parent would only be required to help once every ten weeks.

Hubby is not the volunteering type, particularly when it comes to kid-based activities. It was always me involved with the school activities, organising birthday parties, and so on. But he made the rookie mistake of making eye contact with Mandy and before he knew it, his hand was in the air. He rationalised it by thinking ninety minutes every ten weeks wasn't that bad, plus he would get to spend some time with his son. Unfortunately, he was one of only three volunteers, drastically increasing the frequency of his new commitment. Not that he knew it then, but ultimately that wouldn't matter.

As the first name on the list he was the parent helper on the Beavers' trip to a magic show in the Town Hall the following week. Since the show was open to the public I decided to go along with our daughter. The performance was very much what you would expect of a magic show in the Town Hall of a small town, very much Simon Cowell's worst nightmare. But by far and away the best part of the show was hubby in an authoritative role, trying to corral twenty-nine unruly children who weren't his.

At home hubby is very much bad cop and has always been quite strict with the kids. He felt that if you didn't teach them to be socially aware by a young age then you would miss your chance. This usually presented itself as him losing his shit every time the children misbehaved. But you can't lose your shit with other people's kids, no matter how much they deserve it. So this was the first time either of our kids had witnessed their dad having to deal with bad behaviour without losing his mind.

Sitting two rows back, I could almost feel the rage-fuelled heat coming from his face as he asked the same child, for the tenth time, to stop shouting at the acts when they were performing their tricks. To be fair, the kid was proper heckling, and it can't be easy being a magician at the best of times, let alone when a seven-year-old child is pointing out your poor life choices.

Hubby's temper was pushed further by the sheer volume of trips to the bathroom. As the only male helper he had to do all the toilet runs. One kid went so many times he would have been as well just spending the entire duration of the show in the loo.

The evening was a success, if for no other reason than thirty Beavers left the Scout Hall and thirty Beavers returned alive. And that counts as a victory. I don't know if the magicians would have classed it as a success, though, and I'm sure at least one probably hung up his wand for good that night.

Akela was so impressed with hubby, that she asked him to be a parent helper the following week. Many people who have met him may mistake him for being quite gruff, which he isn't at heart (probably more camp than gruff), the truth is he's too nice and finds it difficult to say no to anybody. Which is why, over the years, he has become a little more distant, as he ends up doing favours for everybody. Cornered, he couldn't say no, and next session he found himself gluing ice-lolly sticks together to make God-knows-what. Towards the end, Mandy asked if she could have a word with him in the kitchen, where she cryptically told him that Christine wanted to speak to him in the office.

This baffled hubby, as he had no idea who Christine was, and the office was literally right next to the kitchen; before he could even consider why Mandy wouldn't have taken him directly to Christine he immediately began to panic. I don't know if he was dropped on his head when he was a baby, but his mind doesn't seem to work properly – his first thought was that a child had falsely accused him of hitting them.

He walked into the office with the look of a guilty man, to be confronted by a large woman, her back to him, standing at a computer.

This is what happened next:

Hubby: 'Hi, Mandy said I was to speak to Christine.'

Christine: 'I'm just putting in an order for uniforms. What size are you?' (Didn't even introduce herself.)

H: 'Oh, sorry. There must be a mistake, I'm just a parent helper. I don't need a uniform.'

C: 'Yeah, Mandy said you were really good at the magic show last week, so you are a leader now.'

At this point hubby, like a normal person, should have said no I'm not, you lunatic, that isn't how life works. He went for a rather different approach.

H: 'Eh, I'm really fat. Deceptively so. I doubt you would get a pair of trousers to fit me.'

C: 'I'm sure I will, what size are you?'

H: 'At least a forty-six-inch waist, honestly I struggle to get trousers anywhere.'

C: 'Nope, not a problem. Look they go up to sixty-inch waist on the website. That's them ordered for you, they'll be here next week.'

When he came home and told me what had happened, I don't know what shocked me most, the fact he hadn't told Christine no, or that you can have a sixty-inch waist and still be a Scout Leader. Surely you would be a shut-in? Either way, out of nothing more than social awkwardness, my then thirty-three-year-old husband was now a Beaver Leader.

The well-read amongst you (or Disney fans) will realise that Akela is the name of the head of the wolf pack in Rudyard Kipling's classic, The Jungle Book.

All Scout leaders are named after characters from the book, and hubby was no different. He was renamed Shere Khan, who you may know was the tiger. Depending on your knowledge of Kipling's work, you may also know that while Akela adopted and raised Mowgli, the human child, Shere Khan did his best to kill and eat him.

I assume the Scout movement is aware of this, and I don't know what message they are trying to send out by naming leaders after a murderous big cat with a taste for children. Perhaps the name is reserved for those leaders who are brought in as enforcers, to scare unruly kids.

Hubby brought home his uniform the following week, which coincided with us having friends over for dinner. Having served dessert, and after much goading, hubby agreed to model his new outfit. Stepping into the room, just as I was putting a spoonful of apple crumble into my mouth, I saw him in all his glory. The sight of him dressed as a giant Boy-Scout, neckerchief and all, made me laugh so hard I inhaled my pudding and began choking.

Even as my eyes bulged out of my head and I fought to catch my breath, I still couldn't avert my gaze. If you have ever seen the Disney Pixar film, Up, he looked like a giant version of Russell. Standing in front of me, as I all but choked to death, it had never been clearer to me why he was a virgin when we first met. I've always had a bit of a thing for guys in uniform, but I was thinking more fireman than man-child. I don't think even Idris Elba could make a woggle sexy.

Luckily, my friend, sitting next to me, thumped me so hard between my shoulder blades that she managed to dislodge the crumble from my throat, allowing me to breathe freely and laugh even harder.

As well as having to dress like a giant Boy-Scout every week, hubby found out that his commitment would stretch to far more than ninety minutes every Thursday. The Beavers had regular sleepovers at the Scout Hall on a Saturday, took part in a giant sleepover once a year which involved every section of the group from Beavers to Explorers, and group camp which was a weekend long camping 'extravaganza'. It was at group camp he would have his investiture, but that was a few weeks away and he was being thrown in at the deep end immediately.

Having already completed three weeks as a parent helper he had some insight as to what to expect but the uniform changed things; he was now both a figure of authority and someone to moan at.

No longer able to hide behind the title of parent helper, now he had to deal with not only the little terrors, but also their parents. Not an easy task when there are so many deluded people out there. He regularly had to reassure parents about their child's safety, even although the kid would spend a large part of each session headbutting walls – a surprisingly common past-time for boys apparently.

One of the most difficult aspects of the role for him was the germs. As an OCD sufferer he struggles with our kids, let alone a hoard of children he isn't related to. And although I do think he can be a little over the top at times with his aversion to germs, I had to concede that the Scout Hall was little more than a swamp of bacteria and viruses. One of the boys was at school with our kids, and on one occasion hubby was stood with his mum at the school gates at home time, when little Stevie came bounding out with chocolate all over his hands.

'Where did you get the chocolate from?' his mum asked.

'It's not chocolate,' he replied. 'I did the toilet and there was no toilet paper, so I used my hands.'

Her child had taken a shit and in lieu of toilet roll, had used his own hands to wipe his bum and, mind-bogglingly, then decided not to wash his hands. His mum's response?

'Oh, what are you like, Stevie?' She chuckled.

Then she let him get in the car. With shit all over his hands. These are real people and they walk amongst us.

Hubby made sure that there was never an opportunity where Stevie could put his hands anywhere near him, or anything he might touch. Not only because of shit-gate, but also because during circle time Stevie would stand with his finger up his own bum rummaging around like a granny in a bag of Werther's Originals.

Before long, group camp rolled around, and hubby was thrilled to learn that the Beavers would only be attending on the Saturday, with the rest of the section camping out from the Friday night till Sunday evening. His investiture was to be carried out alongside three others who had been pressganged – I mean, chosen – to become leaders.

Disaster struck days before the big event, when hubby managed to put a drill through the back of his knuckle and had to have emergency surgery. (Quick side note, a few weeks later when he returned to the hospital to have his stitches checked, he cried, and then puked, and then had to go for a lie down in a dark room. Not to imply that women are tougher, but after giving birth to both children I had to get my vagina stitched, and all I got offered was tea and toast.)

With his arm in a sling, he took solace in the fact that his stupidity would at least get him out of attending group camp. His sense of relief was shattered almost immediately, when Akela told him that without him the Beavers could not attend, as they had a strict adult to child ratio that must be adhered to. She reassured him he wouldn't even need both hands and would purely serve as an observer. With no other choice, he agreed to go.

On the Saturday morning I helped him get dressed and did his little neckie for him, before doing the same for our six-year-old, and I dropped them both off at the Scout Hall to get the bus.

The location for group camp was a large field in the countryside, deep in the woods, and encircled by a river. The bus would take them as far as the perimeter of the forest, and then it was a twenty-minute hike, before finally traipsing down a steep hill. Hubby had been assured by Christine that it was amazing, and that once the leader team were finished setting up it was like a city in the forest.

Christine lied. You can imagine hubby's horror, when after a twenty-minute hike through the woods with sixty Beavers (thirty from a Tuesday night session and thirty from a Thursday night), he was confronted with a field, that up until twenty-four hours before had been used to keep a flock of sheep in. The sheer scale of sheep shit in that field was unbelievable, there was almost as much shit as there was grass.

He immediately questioned what kind of cities Christine had been visiting, or if indeed, she even knew what a city was. Because apparently, she thought two large tents, twenty small tents, two Porta-loos (located at the top of the hill for number twos), and a trench (located at the bottom of the hill for number ones), was enough to obtain city status.

I can personally testify to just how shit it was, both literally and figuratively, as I was there. Not in any official capacity but purely because I wanted to support (laugh at) hubby on his investiture. I also dragged our daughter and my grandparents along for the ride. Not an easy task, walking two septuagenarians through twenty minutes of forest and down a hill into a cesspit of sheep faeces. Particularly because my grandparents refused to wear appropriate clothing, my grampa opting for shirt and tie, and a pair of brogues.

The investiture was even more hilarious than I had hoped and involved various cult-like incantations and dancing. I may be exaggerating slightly, but the highlight was when the Group Scout Leader held out the ceremonial flag pole horizontally, for the new leaders to touch as they took their oath. Unfortunately for hubby, the hand he needed to use was bandaged, and in a sling, something which the Scout Leader didn't seemed to factor in when he held the pole out at arms-length. This meant that hubby had to recite his oath bent over from the waist to reach the pole; from the angle we were at, it looked like he was kissing it. I'm sure quite a lot of people got the impression that he really loved Scouting. Or flag poles.

That couldn't have been farther from the truth. Aside from making some friends with other leaders who had started as parent helpers, he really did not enjoy his time in the pack. He set out to make himself as ineffectual as possible, to the point where almost everybody thought he was completely incompetent. A couple of other leaders saw through his ruse and would try to coax him in to taking on more responsibility. But he was having none of it, he didn't mind getting his hands dirty and doing the manual work required on the night, but he didn't want to become an integral part of the movement, as he knew that as soon as our son left, he would too.

Part of his plan involved repeatedly failing to complete any of the training modules that were required to be a leader. He managed to dodge the first three training modules like a multi-national conglomerate dodges tax, but he got caught one night under the pretence of a leader night out.

Turning up at the hall at the agreed time, he was told they were going to take the Scout minibus to go for drinks a couple of towns over. It was only once they were in motion he learned they were actually going to do some training with other leaders from across the county.

He found himself kidnapped and taken to a church hall in another town – he insisted I use the word 'kidnapped', even though I have told him he is being overly dramatic. Years have passed since this incident and he is just as angry about it now as he was then. The training involved learning about appropriate relationships with children in your care and was pretty much what you would expect of any organisation that is responsible for looking after our youth. To make it a little less dry the organisers got the leaders to do a couple of tasks. One was to go around the room answering questions that had been laid out on tables. Each table had three cups on it, one labelled Yes, one labelled No, and one labelled Maybe. The leaders were given cocktail sticks and had to put a stick in the cup they thought corresponded to the correct response to the question.

One of the questions was, 'Is it okay to have a physical relationship with a child in your care?'

By the time hubby got to that table there were two cocktail sticks in the Maybe cup.

Not only had he been kidnapped, but he was now being held in a church hall with two budding paedos. He spent the rest of the time scanning the hall for potential suspects; worryingly he abandoned this when he identified too many.

What shocked hubby most during his time in the Scout Hall was the amount of sex taking place. Don't panic, I know if you are over a certain age, in the last few years you will have seen so many of your favourite childhood stars come under suspicion, but the sex was between the leaders. In the short time he was there two marriages were ended by Scout Hall affairs, it seemed like the randy buggers were Dyb, Dyb, Dybbing everywhere.

Our son finally quit, shortly after moving up to Cubs, but because he had done it halfway through the year hubby had to see the rest of the year out, which he was just thrilled about.

He kept the uniform, though, and if I'm ever feeling low he'll pop it on for me and give me his best Ging Gang Goolie.

Chapter Thirty-One

Callie

What were you thINKing...

The older you get, the more aware you become of trends. It becomes even more apparent when you are a parent, because no-one buys into a trend quite like children.

For a demographic that have no cash of their own, kids a lot of people very rich. When mine were little it was Moshi Monsters, and I have drawers full of multi-coloured, plastic monsters, that they just had to have. I even have a special drawer for the gold edition Moshis that my son begged for, insisting he would never ask for anything again, if he could just have them.

He didn't seem so keen on them recently, after I brought them out when his friends came around for a Fortnite tournament. Apparently, I am 'soooo embarrassing'.

Fortnite is the current trend, an online shoot 'em up game that teenagers and adults alike are going crazy for. It is basically like Call of Duty for virgins of all ages.

Although children are the ultimate masters of short-lived trends, we are all to an extent guilty of it. Just look at fashion. I'm pretty sure that what you are wearing now is not what you were wearing twenty years ago. Unless you are like my husband.

He is the antithesis of trendy. He has played the long game, realising in his mid-teens that all the adults he knew looked back at old photos of themselves and cringed at their appearance. He noted that not only would they comment on their clothes, but more markedly their hairstyle. So, he shaved his head and has dressed exclusively in black t-shirt and jeans ever since. If you were to put all the photos of him together in chronological order and flick through them like a flip book, you wouldn't be able to tell the difference. Well, aside from the fact he has doubled his own body weight. It would look like a picture story about a man that had an air hose shoved up his arse and is going to eventually explode. The style of his clothes may have remained constant, but the amount of material required to make them has increased drastically.

In the interests of balance, I must admit to having a few howlers in my own closet –literally and figuratively. One of my regular clubbing outfits in the 1990s was a silk Japanese kimono, which may have been a little small for someone nearly six-feet tall. With hindsight, it might have gone well with my mother-in-law's jacket from TK Maxx.

Whilst toys may be expensive and under-appreciated, and fashion faux-pas' may be embarrassing, at least they are both temporary. One trend that leaves an indelible mark is the tattoo. Before anybody starts to get their hackles up because they think I'm about to badmouth tattoos, calm down, I'm not the judgemental type and it would be hypocritical because I have two of my own.

Not that I am happy with either of them. The first, Winnie the Pooh, was done when I was eighteen and exceptionally drunk. It was very much a 'fuck you' to my father, who despite being a physically abusive alcoholic deadbeat, had a very pious attitude towards getting inked.

The second was done on a whim, but considerably more sophisticated. At least I thought it was. What I wanted was the Fibonacci Sequence, which is a series of numbers, i.e. 0,1,1,2,3,5,8,13,21,34...The next number is found by adding the two numbers before it, so the next number in the sequence would be 55, and so on. When you make squares with those widths you get a beautiful spiral shape, and that is what I got tattooed on my back. What I hadn't considered was that most people don't know what the Fibonacci Sequence is, or what its physical representation looks like. So, when people saw my tattoo, they always said the same thing, 'Oh, do you like Charles Rennie Mackintosh?'

Mr Mackintosh was a Scottish architect and designer with a style that could be mistaken for Fibonacci, and while I have nothing against him or his work, I certainly wouldn't have had it tattooed on my back. After several failed attempts at trying to explain to inquisitive strangers what the Fibonacci Sequence is, I gave up, and just said I was a big fan of Mackintosh. In all the years I have had it, two people have guessed correctly as to what it is.

Hubby takes great delight in this, as he was not in favour of me getting it in the first place. He doesn't have a problem with tattoos per se, but he doesn't see the point in getting one just for the sake of it. He, of course, is ink free, and I imagine if he were ever to get one it would be of a Staedtler ruler or some Post-It Notes, or something equally boring.

Whilst I have some regrets about my choice of tats, it pales into insignificance compared to my client Callie.

If you were to meet Callie on the beach, wearing a bikini, you would never know she had any tattoos. That is because Callie's three tattoos are all somewhere very personal, with one of them located in a place I didn't even know you could get tattooed.

When most people are dipping their toe into getting inked for the first time, they usually go for something on the arm or shoulder, perhaps the foot if they are the adventurous type. Callie went all in and got her first tattoo on her labia – yep, that's right, she got a twatoo.

And what's worse than getting a tattoo on your fanny? Getting a tattoo of your boyfriend's name on your fanny.

If any young ladies are reading this, then please accept the wisdom of someone a bit longer in the tooth: if your boyfriend suggests you get his name inked onto your vagina – get rid of him.

It is a lot more difficult and takes a lot longer to get rid of a tattoo than it does an arsehole. What kind of man convinces a young woman to mark her genitals with his name? And for what reason? To let other guys know she is taken? That's the most flawed system for ensuring monogamy I have ever heard of.

'Right, love, if any guys come around looking to get into your knickers when I'm not here, just show them your fanny and they'll get the message.'

The only positive I can gleam from this situation is that Callie's boyfriend's name was Rob, had it been Jonathon she might have run out of lip.

If you are a romantic, you may find it upsetting to learn that Callie and her beau didn't last, *quelle surprise*. Who could have envisaged that this modern-day Romeo and Juliet wouldn't live happily ever after?

At least Callie had learned a valuable lesson and would never get another man's name tattooed on her body.

Er, not really, because apparently Callie has a type. And that type is a human turd. The next boyfriend struggled to come to terms with the fact that she had another man's name on her vagina. Not out of concern for her and any violation of her inherent human rights, but because he was her new owner, sorry, *partner*, who I imagine, was the kind of guy who goes to Ibiza with the lads, all adorned in matching t-shirts with witty slogans like 'Pussy Patrol', hunting girls that are too drunk to make good decisions. The only way his ego could handle Callie's perceived slight was to brand her again. Her second tattoo was placed in the middle of her pubic thatch, proudly displaying her new master.

I am aware it looks like I'm absolving Callie of any responsibility, but she was very young and vulnerable, and these guys were a lot older. Not to mention, bell-ends.

You may have already guessed where this is going, and you would be right, another relationship on the scrapheap and another lucky escape for Callie. Alexander Graham Bell famously said, 'When one door closes another door opens…' but I don't think he was expecting an even bigger arsehole to be behind that open door. Nothing if not consistent, Callie found herself in yet another dysfunctional relationship with Donald arguably an even bigger bellend. And guess what, he wanted to leave his stamp on her too, but he aspired to greater things. Not satisfied with just his name in her pubic thatch, he had a crown put above it to distinguish himself from the plebs that came before him.

At this point you could be forgiven for thinking none of this is particularly funny, and you would be right. The funny part happened when he came with Callie to her waxing appointment.

Donald's nose was put out of joint immediately when he tried to follow Callie into the treatment room, and I explained to him in no uncertain terms that he would remain in the waiting room until the treatment was finished. Clearly, he was not used to being spoken to in such a manner by a lowly woman, and anger was etched across his face as he sat down.

This was the first time that I had seen Callie since her new tattoo and I fought hard not to say anything when I saw DONALD in bold letters, with a shoddy crown above it. I had long given up on trying to dissuade her from getting any more ink.

'What do you think of her new tat?' Donald sneered, when we came out of the treatment room.

Referring to Callie as 'her' was a red rag to a bull and I let my temper get the better of me.

'Yeah nice, I particularly like the crown. So, what does that make you? King Fanny?' I retorted.

Donald did not like that one bit and shot up from his seat in a rage. 'Who the fuck d'you think you're talking to, you snooty bitch?' he spat, waving his arms about and sticking his chest out like a paper gangster.

Before I even had the chance to open my mouth to respond, I was distracted by a flurry of movement in my peripheral vision. Like a fat Jack-in-the-box on speed, hubby had swung round the doorframe of his office and thwacked Donald across the face with a shatterproof ruler. The noise was remarkable.

What was even more remarkable, was that he followed this up by saying, 'Off you fuck', like a giant, angry, Yoda.

This was very much out of character for hubby – the slap, that is, and not the Yoda impersonation – as he never advocates violence. But he knew of Donald, and of his quick hands with women, so he rode into action with his sword of plastic. He may not be a fighter, but his sheer bulk was enough to put the shitters up Donald, and I thoroughly enjoyed every moment of it as the loser scuttled away.

The power might have gone to hubby's head slightly. He started referring to his ruler as the 'enforcer' and hung it on a hook by his office door 'just in case'. I think he must have been concerned he had done something that might be considered sexy, so he had to redress the balance.

Happily, I can instil some faith back in the romantics among you, the story has a happy ending.

After seeing hubby jump to my defence Callie had an epiphany. She realised she should be with someone who would protect her, rather than abuse her, and King Donald was given his marching orders.

I have a very good friend who does laser tattoo removal and I arranged for Callie to have her ink erased. It was certainly a first for me – having three cocks removed from a client's vagina.

Callie is now happily married to a great guy and they are having their first baby this year.

Chapter Thirty-Two

Ross

What would mama say...

At the risk of sounding like a relic, one of my biggest worries as a parent is smartphones. While I understand they are a remarkable development, with countless real-world applications, I can't help but feel they are producing a generation of disengaged zombies.

The school run in the morning is like being an extra in The Walking Dead: hordes of teens walking out in front of moving cars, their eyes glued to whatever hilarious memes are doing the rounds that day. Incidentally, if you are over thirty and want a laugh, then try pronouncing the word meme around a group of teenagers and watch them collectively lose their minds at how wrong you get it. I do it as a hobby.

The biggest use for these phones, that have more technology than it took to put man on the moon, seems to be social media, which until recently I thought consisted of Facebook and Twitter. How wrong I was. There's Instagram, Reddit, Tumblr, Monkey, Snapchat, Whatsapp, and on, and on. They market themselves to the youth of today with statements like '...a place to express yourself, discover yourself and bond over the stuff you love.'

Far be it for me to suggest we should limit teenagers' expression online, but a substantial number of them seem to have interpreted this expression as sending sexually explicit photos of themselves to each other. So prevalent is the request to 'send nudes' from young men to young women, that it has become a punchline in many online jokes. Boys are straight up asking girls to send them naked pictures of themselves, with the kind of casual approach you would ask someone how their day is going.

That is another problem with mobile phones and social media, it puts a physical distance between people that allows them to say things they would never say in person. When I was at school, if a boy walked up to a girl and said, 'Show us your tits,' he would get a slap in the face. But now girls are not only tolerating this kind of behaviour but are obliging, because from the safety of their own bedroom they don't perceive the real danger they are in.

Kids aren't mature enough to fully appreciate that anything they say or do online is out there forever. And while they may not care about that when they are young and daft, it can come back to bite them on the arse years later. I spend a lot of time with both my son and daughter explaining the ramifications of their online behaviour, and why it is important to present themselves properly, no matter the forum. Added to that the sheer scale of creeps and perverts on the internet, it is a real concern for parents today.

I was blown away by the number of grown men who will join chat roulette style sites and openly masturbate in front of teenage children. Worryingly, kids now seem so unaffected by this type of behaviour that it doesn't even register. I have had conversations with teenage girls who think it nothing more than a bit of a laugh. These guys are perverts, utilising technology in order to satisfy their sick sexual urges. I wish my daughter didn't have to even give this kind of behaviour a second thought, not during her childhood, anyway. As an adult, doing the job I do, I have had my fair share of run-ins with these types of sickos and I know exactly how to deal with them. Although I have very rarely encountered a client being inappropriate during an appointment, it is not uncommon to be contacted by weirdos who want to drag you into a conversation about their penis.

They very rarely phone, preferring to coax you into a volley of texts that start off perfectly normally, and then become increasingly sexual. It becomes apparent almost immediately when you are dealing with a time-wasting pervert, and most of them can be dealt with simply by telling them they might prefer to contact another waxer, and that's the end of it.

Occasionally, you come across a more determined perv who just won't take the hint. The worst offender I have had the displeasure of dealing with was a young man called Ross. He started off with a simple text inquiry about male intimate waxing, then showed his true intentions in his second message, explaining to me he was getting waxed for his new job as a stripper.

Whilst this may not seem overtly creepy, it's a passive aggressive way of talking about taking his clothes off, which opens the door to talk about other things. At this stage in communicating with a new client who has set off alarm bells, I always remain professional and bring the topic back to the treatment, giving them the benefit of the doubt on the off-chance that they simply aren't presenting themselves very well.

Ross made this very difficult with a follow up message, explaining he was nervous about his new job, as he didn't know how they would handle him having such a massive cock. I don't know what I was meant to do with that information, swoon and applaud him for having a penis, I assume. However, I chose to ignore his boast, responding with some practical advice regarding the treatment.

Ross ploughed on regardless, advising me that his penis was so large he didn't know how I would be able to wax it. Admittedly this threw me as I also wax legs, and I couldn't begin to comprehend a penis so large it would prove to be logistically more difficult than an entire leg. I responded one last time, again ignoring his magnificent claims and bringing the chat back to waxing. This seemed to do the trick as Ross stopped messaging and I chalked it up to nothing more than a waste of ten minutes of my life.

If only it was that easy. The following night, having just finished work, I flopped onto the couch and my phone pinged. Ross had very kindly sent me a photo of himself naked. This may surprise those of you who have a mental image of what Ross may look like, but he was a very attractive young man, with a well-muscled physique. Not the creepy-looking weirdo you imagine indulges in this kind of behaviour because he can't talk to women in the real world.

Before I could even process what had just happened, my phone pinged again, this time with a photo of Ross naked, with an erection. Regarding his claim of having a massive penis, I can confirm that he wasn't lying, and whilst it was very large it certainly wasn't the size of a leg. I was furious that he had the audacity to think he could send me unsolicited photos of that nature. I am no wallflower and am certainly not easily shocked, but who the hell did this guy think he was, sending sexually explicit images to a woman he had never met. And what the hell did he expect to come of it?

If I was angry, hubby was apoplectic and began sharpening the 'enforcer' into a shiv, saying things about 'having a straightener.' He had watched a Danny Dyer film the night before and can be extremely suggestible because the only straightener he has ever been involved with are the ones I use for my hair when he helps me do the back of my head.

I calmed hubby down by putting The Goonies on, and let his mind drift to becoming a treasure hunter with his group of misfit friends. (He probably imagined he would be Mikey, but really, he would be Chunk.)

I calmed myself down by imagining hubby doing the truffle shuffle, and then I set about teaching Ross an important lesson in not fucking about with women. He was not only stupid enough to include his face in both photos, but he also provided me with his full name. If you think that I should have reported him to the police, then you are a far nicer person than me. If a guy like that gets reported to the police, he will get a slap on the wrist and move on to the next unsuspecting woman. No, I used woman power. I logged into my Facebook account and, with a simple search, found Ross. I then searched his friends list for every woman with the same surname as him; this included his mum, sisters, aunts, and cousins. I then forwarded them the photos with the following message:

Hi ladies, sorry to have to do this, but Ross contacted me about waxing and then sent me unsolicited photos of himself, both naked and in a state of arousal. He clearly thinks that this is an acceptable thing to do to a woman he has never met, so I'm sure he doesn't mind you guys seeing them. You may want to speak to him about acceptable behaviour with members of the opposite sex. Thanks, Mona.

I received an apology from Ross almost immediately, as well as from his mum and one of his sisters, who had also showed the message to Ross' girlfriend. The trauma of his mum seeing him with a stiffy will stay with Ross, long after the effect of a police warning would have worn off. From what I could gather the reaction he received from most of the family left him out in the cold, to say the least. So, in honour of Ross, I've done him a wee limerick:

There once was a lad with a big willy.
His decision to show me was silly.
Regrets he had some.
When I showed his mum.
And the reception he got was chilly.

Chapter Thirty-Three

Veronica

Good vibrations...

The humble AA battery is often taken for granted. By far and away the most popular of disposable batteries – with some sources citing it as outselling AAAs at a ratio of 10:1 – it has been a mainstay in houses across the world for decades.

If your home is anything like mine you will use AAs for anything from TV remotes to alarm sensors, games console controllers to wall clocks. And if you, like me, are over a certain age then you probably have a stash somewhere in a kitchen drawer in case of emergencies – such as for the trusty torch safely stored in the kitchen cupboard, waiting patiently in the event of a power cut. It seemed like power cuts were all the rage in the UK in the 20th century. They're not so popular now; my children have only experienced one in their lifetime and they cried like it was the beginning of the apocalypse. I think they were expecting to hear the siren from *The Purge* announcing their impending death. Then the real tears started when they realised, they faced a far graver reality: no Wi-Fi.

The AA was introduced in 1907 by The American Ever Ready Company (you may know them better as Energizer) and forty years later the American National Standards Institute standardised the size with which we are all familiar today.

In 1957, three Ever Ready employees invented a long-lasting alkaline battery. However, as the company failed to proactively market their new product in favour of pushing the original zinc-carbon battery, they lost a sizeable share of the market to competitor, Duracell.

Fun fact: both Energizer and Duracell have used pink bunnies in their marketing campaigns. Duracell used the mascot first, back in the early 70's, going on to trademark the little fellow when the ad campaign became a success. When the company allowed the trademark on the brightly-coloured critter to lapse in the late 80's Energizer saw an opportunity and introduced their own battery-powered pink hopper. As you can imagine, this led to some charged legal action between the two companies followed by an out-of-court settlement.

Double fun fact: both Energizer and Duracell's alkaline AA batteries are suitable for use in the Rampant Rabbit (no relation to either the Energizer or Duracell bunnies), currently available on Amazon for £48.00. However, you may want to consider how effective they are as a power source if you are to believe the one-star review left by Mr Joe Cooke, UK:

1.0 out of 5 stars **Total garbage**

Reviewed in the United Kingdom on 26 July 2023

Verified Purchase

Treated my Mrs to this total rubbish played with cheaper ones great fun this did nothing runs on 3 pencil batteries not enough power the noise it makes puts her off and just dod nothing for her 3 second orgasm got to be kidding .Don't waste your money .

I can't speak to the noise, but I think I would be more put off by Mr Cooke's grammar, punctuation, and spelling, particularly as Amazon has a spellcheck function on its review option. Nonetheless, my thoughts go out to Mrs Cooke and her '3 second orgasm'.

But Mona, why are you banging on about AA batteries, I hear you ask? What do AA batteries have to do with intimate waxing? And the answer is, nothing. AA batteries have nothing to do with intimate waxing. Normally.

My client Veronica is very normal. She is an office worker for a local Council, she lives in a two-bed mid-terrace villa with her fiancé, and she likes to bake in her spare time. Normal.

One Tuesday, Veronica was in with me for her usual Hollywood appointment. She had stripped off and assumed the smear position on the treatment bed, ready to begin. If you aren't familiar with the smear position, it means legs bent, feet together, knees apart.

As I approached the bed, twirling a wooden spatula of hot wax, Veronica covered her mouth and let out a sharp cough. As a result of the exertion a small cylindrical object was partially pushed out from her vagina.

'Oh my god, a battery just came out of my fanny, didn't it?' she asked, having seen the look of shock on my face.

Veronica was correct. A battery was indeed half hanging out of her vag. Not normal. Instinctively I pulled it out and held the AA aloft as we both inspected it.

'I've been looking for that for days,' she explained.

'In your vagina?' I asked confused.

'Obviously not.' She sighed. 'I didn't realise it was inside me.'

Veronica went on to explain that the week before she had been on a video call with her fiancé, who worked away on an oil rig for half the month. The call soon became amorous, and the pair indulged in a somewhat energetic round of phone sex. At some point Veronica decided to spice up proceedings using a sex toy, namely a vibrator.

As we have already touched on at various points, the world of sex toys is both wide and varied. So, for the purpose of clarity I will highlight an important difference between two specific categories of vibrators. Firstly, we have the dildo vibrator, which has the shape and appearance of a penis (some more realistic-looking than others) and is designed to be inserted into the vagina. Secondly, we have the clitoral stimulator vibrator, found in various shapes, though not the shape or appearance of a penis, and it is not designed to be inserted into the vagina. A third option combines the two: a vibrating dildo with a built-in clitoral stimulator. An example of this is the Rampant Rabbit that failed so disastrously to satisfy Mrs Cooke.

Veronica had been using a clitoral stimulator, however, in the throes of passion she got carried away and shoved it inside herself like a dildo. Big no-no. One of the key differences between the two devices is how the batteries are stored. Dildo vibrators often use a twist and lock mechanism at the base of the device, not dissimilar to a torch. Clitoral stimulators, however, have no such need for a secure storage compartment and can use a simple click-cover, like a TV remote.

And it was as Vibrating Veronica was pounding away at herself that the cover came loose, and the battery became lodged inside her vagina.

There may be some among you (I'm looking at the men), who think it unlikely that a woman could have a foreign object inside their vagina and be completely unaware of it. Well, you would be wrong.

I had a friend who went out for dinner with her then boyfriend and when they were seated at their table, she noticed a dreadful odour. She complained to the waiter and asked that they be moved, which they were. She found the smell to be equally bad at the second table, so she left the restaurant in disgust. It was only when she was in the bathroom later that night she discovered a forgotten tampon inside her that had been there for some considerable time. *She* was the smell.

When I offered the battery back to Veronica, which seemed to be in good condition despite its ordeal, she politely declined and asked me to dispose of it. So, I set it aside on a tissue to put it in the appropriate recycling bin later, and I finished her wax.

Imagine my surprise later in the day when I returned to find the battery missing.

The case of the missing battery didn't remain open for long. Hubby told me later that day he had taken the AA from my workroom for his new tabletop calculator. I didn't have the heart to tell him where it had come from. He then proceeded to waste twenty minutes of my life telling me about all the 'cool' functions his new calculator had, and I couldn't help but think how fitting it was that the battery had gone from one fanny to another.

Chapter Thirty-Four

Hubby

The butt of the joke...

Hubby has always been a good sport when it comes to being a guinea-pig for new types of wax. Whether it is strip wax or hot wax he usually volunteers as tribute, with a small amount of cajoling.

I have always used the same high-end, French brand of hot wax and have never been anything other than 100% happy with it. Despite this, I don't feel like I would be doing my job properly if I didn't test every new product on the market. As a result, hubby has now had his legs and dangly bits waxed so often it isn't really an issue for him.

The one treatment I could never get him to agree to, though, was an eyebrow wax. He always maintained this was too much a lady's treatment. I thought he was secretly worried I would rip his entire eyebrow off for a laugh – which granted would be hilarious, but completely unprofessional and not something I would ever do. Even if I was pissed off with him.

He is such a good sport, that when my young cousin came to do work experience with me, as part of her beauty diploma, he agreed to be a model for a lower-leg wax. That may not seem like such a big deal, given the frequency with which he had been waxed, but having a treatment from a relative novice is a completely different experience.

Whilst he was distracted getting his leg waxed, I seized the opportunity to suggest I do an eyebrow wax at the same time. I won't lie, he wasn't keen, so I had to point out that he didn't really have eyebrows anymore, as he had hairs growing out of his forehead. He was beginning to look like a very chubby Teen-Wolf. It didn't really have the desired effect, because he just doesn't care about his appearance, and is a big fan of Michael J. Fox. The thing that swung it for him was when I pointed out how efficient it would be having the two treatments done at the same time. That's how much of a dweeb he is, agreeing to have not one, but two treatments done that he didn't want, purely because it appealed to his desire to use time effectively.

I have never been more excited to do a treatment on anyone, as not only was I planning to tidy up his brows, I was also going to tint them. He wouldn't even understand the concept of tinting eyebrows, but he desperately needed them done, because although his brows were growing up onto his forehead, they were simultaneously thinning at the sides. So by the time his legs were finished, he had perfectly groomed eyebrows, which I thought massively improved his face. When I handed him the mirror, he wasn't so keen.

'Bloody hell, what have you done?' he wailed. 'I look like David Gandy.'

'Oh, babe,' I replied. 'David Brent at best.' And my cousin and I laughed.

Bizarrely, hubby took that as a compliment because he is a massive fan of Brent in The Office. There is a scene in one of the episodes, where office joker Tim puts co-worker Gareth's stapler in a jelly. Hubby nearly shit himself laughing at that; I imagine he would have really soiled himself if it had been a ruler instead of a stapler.

Hubby and I are regularly the butt of each other's jokes, and I think the key to a long marriage is not only to be able to laugh with each other, but also at each other. It is something we have tried to instil in our kids, that laughter is a good thing and whether people are laughing with you or at you – just join in and find the funny.

I enjoy laughing at hubby so much that the final story in my diary is about him, I hope you enjoy it as much as I do.

Aunt Isa, the Destroyer of Desserts, spent the last few months of her life in a care home, where we visited as often as possible. It was a nice facility, each resident getting their own apartment-style accommodation, with bedroom, living area, wet-room and kitchen – albeit with no oven or hob. Each wing had a common area with lounge, dining area and kitchen, in which the residents were encouraged to spend time interacting.

Hubby, the kids, and I, got to know most of Aunt Isa's neighbours to say hello to as we passed them in the hallways. Conversations didn't tend to go much further than that, as all of them had dementia at one stage or another.

On one occasion, hubby and the kids were visiting Aunt Isa, and had just settled onto the sofas when the letterbox on her door began rattling. I always thought it strange the residents had letterboxes, as any post received was delivered to the reception desk of the facility and then handed out by the staff. I assume it was to maintain a sense of normality.

'There's that bloody woman again,' Aunt Isa exclaimed.

The bloody woman in question was Joy, Isa's arch-enemy.

Joy looked like every old woman from every horror film ever made. She had a stoop so severe she was almost bent double, and her deathly thin frame, with elongated, bony limbs and fingers gave her the appearance of a witch. She had never spoken to any of us directly, but Isa and Joy had beef from the common area, neither of them could remember why, though, because of the dementia.

'Go away, you stupid old woman,' Aunt Isa shouted.

Hubby placated Isa before going to speak to Joy. As he opened the door, she grabbed his hand with surprising speed.

'It's you I want,' Joy said, stroking his fingers.

'Sorry, Joy, we're up to see Aunt Isa,' hubby replied.

'She doesn't know what she's doing,' Joy spat, peering round hubby at Isa.

'Get away, stupid woman,' Isa shouted from across the room.

'Joy, Aunt Isa is very nice to us, and we are up to spend some time with her, if you don't mind,' hubby explained softly, pulling his hand away gently, before closing the door.

Just as he got back to his seat, he could hear Joy in the corridor saying, 'Help,' over and over.

Not wanting to leave her in distress, he returned to the door and as soon as he opened it, she surged forward and grabbed him.

'It's you I want. It's you I want. It's you I want,' she repeated, like an incantation.

With Isa's rage reaching Hulk-like levels, and Joy seeming completely disorientated, hubby thought the best thing to do was find a member of staff. As he guided Joy down the corridor, she stroked his left forearm with her right hand.

'It's you I want. It's you I want. It's you I want.'

Turning left into the main corridor, they slowly made their way towards the common area. As they approached, hubby was able to make eye-contact with one of the staff and mouthed, 'Help.'

'It's you I want. It's you I want. It's you I want.'

As the carer walked towards them, smiling at hubby, Joy suddenly shoved her right hand down his pants and grabbed his arse.

'It's him I want,' Joy said to the carer.

And suddenly the penny dropped, and hubby realised how naïve he had been. Joy groped his buttock like she was kneading dough, her fingers dangerously close to carrying out a prostate exam. The carer was none the wiser, as she couldn't see what Joy was up to from the front.

'Come on, Joy, that young man is here to see Isa,' the carer said softly.

'It's him I want,' Joy continued. 'He's the best at it. All the girls say so. He really knows what he's doing. It's him I want.'

I don't want to rain on his parade, and I don't know what girls Joy had been talking to, but hubby barely knows what he's doing. To be honest, it's a bloody miracle we've even managed to have two kids.

In order to get out of his predicament he had to indulge in a spot of impromptu role play, the carer encouraging him to let Joy believe he was her husband, who had to go to work, promising to be home later.

When he returned to Isa's room, he had to keep the incident to himself. Firstly, so as not too enrage Aunt Isa to a point where she might attack Joy, and secondly, because that's not the sort of thing you tell your young children. He had to wait until later in the day, to tell Gran and I about being molested by an octogenarian sex-pest. I think I can speak for Gran when I say that we were both a little dubious. Not that either of us think hubby is a liar, it just seemed a little far-fetched.

Any doubts we had were shattered the next day when we all visited Aunt Isa again. Having arrived early, Isa was still eating her breakfast, which gave us an opportunity to talk to the staff about her care.

As we were talking, Joy appeared from her room to our right, and like a scene from West Side Story, Aunt Isa appeared to our left. Isa spotted her nemesis first, shifting up a gear with her Zimmer-frame, increasing her speed to a slow shuffle.

Joy wasn't interested in Isa, though, having spotted hubby. 'It's him I want. It's him I want,' she repeated.

Anticipating what was about to happen, hubby took Aunt Isa's arm and ushered her and the kids towards her room. But Joy was faster than Isa and cut them off at the pass, positioning herself just in front of Isa's door.

'It's him I want. It's him I want. It's him I want.'

Just before they reached the safety of Isa's room, Joy dropped her trousers revealing a massive pair of rubber incontinence pants.

'MONA, a little help,' I heard hubby exclaim, just as he got Isa and the kids across the threshold.

'It's him I want. It's him I want. It's him I want.'

Hubby was fortunate enough to avert his gaze, sadly I can't say the same. I turned just in time to see Joy's massive rubber pants hit the ground as she began shuffling towards hubby.

There are some things you wish you had never seen, and for me Joy's vagina is one of them. A combination of age and what I can only imagine was a serious sexual appetite in her youth, had resulted in some serious architectural damage to her old lady garden. If she was as game in her youth as she was in her twilight years, she must have had more troops inside her during the war years, than HMS Nelson.

The saddest part of this story is that hubby took it as a reassurance that he has 'still got it'. By 'it' I can only assume he means the ability to attract a mentally impaired, incontinent pensioner. And if that's the case, why the hell would you ever want to have 'it'. Although, worryingly, hubby did start visiting Aunt Isa a lot more often after that. *

*Hubby has demanded I clarify that he did not have, or attempt to have, sex with Joy. Personally, I think he doth protest too much, but as the reader, you can make up your own mind.

Chapter Thirty-Five

Mona

That's all folks...

There has never really been anything that could be considered normal about my life, from my shitty childhood, to my bigger than average height and even bigger mouth, and, of course, spending all day waxing people's genitals. But life is too short to be normal and I love my job.

In the introduction, I stated there was no lesson to be learned, or moral to be taken, from the stories in my diary – and I stand by that. These days, there are too many people, groups, TV-shows, self-help books, doctors etc, telling you how to live your life. And personally, I think it is all a little too much. There is no perfect in this world, we are all just muddling through, doing our best to get by.

I don't know what it is like to walk in your shoes, nor you mine, but the one thing we all have in common is laughter.

Sweet, beautiful, laughter that soothes the soul. Try and surround yourself with people that make you laugh and do your best to make others laugh too. I promise it will make your day a little easier.

Thank you for joining me in my secret diary, I hope you found the funny in these pages. Anyway, the wax pots are calling, so it's time to get back to work.

But I will leave you with this. The next time you are feeling low and life isn't going to plan, just remember that somewhere in a basement in central London there is a man dressed as a rabbit with a carrot up his arse.

Printed in Dunstable, United Kingdom

75520907R00184